Theology and the Scientific Study of Religion

THE LUTHERAN STUDIES SERIES

Volume Two

THEOLOGY AND THE SCIENTIFIC STUDY OF RELIGION

By PAUL L. HOLMER

The Divinity School, Yale University

Publishers

T. S. DENISON & COMPANY, INC.

Minneapolis

Copyright ©, 1961, by
LUTHERAN STUDIES, INC.

Printed in the U. S. A.
By THE BRINGS PRESS

International Copyright Secured
Library of Congress Catalog Card Number: 61-18613

Introduction

This volume is one of a series called *Lutheran Studies*. This series, and each volume within it, seeks to give a hearing to scholars within the Christian Church, and the Lutheran Church in particular, who have found that their learning and research somehow relates to the life and beliefs of Christian people.

It is widely alleged in the twentieth century that detailed scholarship in many fields has rendered Christian theological views impossible and even false. Certain theologians have sometimes spoken categorically too, suggesting that these conflicts in loyalty and belief are clearly matters of sin and unbelief. However these matters ultimately will stand, this series of books is born of the conviction that the real or apparent conflicts between learning and faith must be resolved through detailed scholarship and considered judgment and by persons whose training and experience are sufficient to permit them to weigh the evidence, to assess the argument, and to draw conclusions in a responsible and measured manner.

A book like this one and those to follow are, after all, characteristic expressions of the Christian faith and of Lutheranism. The Protestant Reformation came in large part out of the work and experiences of university professors at Wittenberg, who courageously faced the intellectual and spiritual problems of their day and worked together to make their witness known. The Christian Church has similar resources today in the witness and integrity of its scholars, many of whom are, by virtue of their vocation and place of employment, outside of the orbit of religious orders and institutions. *Lutheran Studies* hopes to encourage these men and women to declare their needs, and to speak their minds to the end that the Christian message will ever be kept clear and the body of Christian believers strengthened. It is probably true that the scholars who speak out of the matrix of learning that appears secular, need the ear and fellowship of other believers and Lutheranism sometimes needs this kind of voice to stir its sluggish consciousness again.

This series was created initially by the action, in 1957, of the two campus pastors of the Lutheran Church (Missouri Synod) and the National Lutheran Council who were then at the University of Minnesota. They arranged for lectures to be delivered to interested parish pastors of the Twin City area by Lutheran professors whose teaching and research were in areas relevant to Christian faith, practice, and doctrine. As the lectures progressed, a concern grew up that these findings, which seemed timely, vital, and even necessary to the pastors, might be made available in a more permanent form for pastors and lay people, students and teachers, and in a larger geographical area. Further discussion led to the incorporation of *Lutheran Studies* as a nonprofit corporation. *Lutheran Studies,* of which this book is the second volume, is being helped by substantial contributions from the benevolence funds of Lutheran Brotherhood Insurance Society of Minneapolis, in the expectation that eventually the project will be self-supporting.

It is hoped that two or three volumes of *Lutheran Studies* will be published each year. In accord with the purposes declared in its articles of incorporation, *Lutheran Studies* seeks to publish and to distribute volumes which will promote and encourage knowledge of the Lutheran faith, stimulate theological scholarship, and feed those kinds of educational and scientific concerns essential to theology and Christian practice. Accordingly volumes are projected on physical science, on contemporary philosophy, on the urban church and the sociology of the city, on some contemporary theologians, on the relationships between recent developmental psychology and the problem of Christian education, and other topics.

These are volumes of inquiry. They do not represent final positions upon the difficult matters which they assess. They are presented in the interest of "clarification" of the issues, of furthering discussion and study, albeit with the hope that the faith which overcomes the world might thereby abound.

REV. REUBEN C. BEISEL
President, St. John's College
Winfield, Kansas

LAWRENCE M. BRINGS
President, Minnesota
Protestant Foundation
Treasurer, *Lutheran Studies*

DR. ARMIN GRAMS
*Professor of Child
Development and Welfare*
University of Minnesota

DR. GEORGE F. HALL
*Campus Pastor for National
Lutheran Council students*
University of Minnesota
President, *Lutheran Studies*

DR. PAUL L. HOLMER
*Professor of Historical
Theology*
Divinity School
Yale University
New Haven, Connecticut

REV. HARRY N. HUXHOLD
Campus Pastor
The Lutheran Church
(Missouri Synod)
University of Minnesota

DR. ARTHUR L. JOHNSON
Professor of Sociology
University of Minnesota
Secretary, *Lutheran Studies*

DR. ROBERT F. SPENCER
Professor of Anthropology
University of Minnesota

DR. ALDERT VAN DER ZIEL
*Professor of Electrical
Engineering*
University of Minnesota
Vice President,
Lutheran Studies

CONTENTS

Preface

This volume tries to make clear a distinction between the learning about religious matters and the learning (and language) that flows forth from the religious life. It is not enough to say that the Christian faith requires only a way of life or a set of attitudes. After all, there is too much said about doctrine, even too much said on its behalf, by those who are the saints and models of the Christian life to allow such a cavalierish rejection. Leo Tolstoy, whose books are so rich with evocative pages on behalf of what he called religious perception, also was one of the most stringent critics of theology and doctrine. Tolstoy and Quakers, pietists and Adolf Harnack, existentialists and positivists, Immanuel Kant and many pastors, have seemed to converge on the thought that the most important matters of faith can not be expressed in learning and language. Again and again, serious and devoted followers of Jesus have looked at the language of faith, both the informal and casual expressions, on the one side, and the more carefully wrought formulations, on the other, as if they were but poor and inappropriate coins in the divine realm.

Certainly it is true that religious faith is also a matter of passion, of attitude, and of obedience. Those of us who talk too easily must admit that the lives of the Apostles and of the saints are a telling rebuke to our verbal facility. Lately though, another kind of attack has come upon the theological and doctrinal front. For today there are some who say that religious language is only emotive, if not completely meaningless. It then becomes tempting to retire altogether, leaving the doctrinal and time-honored language behind as the artifact of an earlier day.

But, in this very breach, religious scholarship has assumed a promising role. From a wide variety of disciplines there have erupted all kinds of new truths about the things of faith. It now becomes tempting—for the learned and sophisticated ones—

to let these new scientific methods, these contemporary disciplined ways of making old things speak, these refurbished inquiries into Scripture, ideas, God, and church, furnish the new "grundlich" stuff of religious affirmation. It will be here argued that this is an egregious error.

Surely it is too much to ask that scientific study, even in the modest Germanic sense of the term meaning orderly and systematic, let alone the stronger Anglo-American sense of the term, do much more than satisfy the demands of intelligence and alleviate the thirst for knowledge. If a man needs the consolation of an abiding conviction, if he cries out for God, then, I would suppose, the words of Paul of Tarsus are still appropriate: "You need not say in your heart, 'Who could go up to Heaven to bring Christ down to us, or who could descend into the depths to bring Him up from the dead?' For the secret is very near you, in your own heart, in your own mouth!"[1] But, the way around is circuitous and a little long. For modern scholarly and scientific studies do help us, not least in this very day. Within a variety of such studies it becomes increasingly clear that there is indeed a language of faith, different in kind and scope from both the everyday patois and the language of scientific study. To see this is in part the purpose of these pages.

It rests with me to record my thanks to students and pastors who listened to two series of lectures on these themes at Luther Hall, St. Paul Campus of the University of Minnesota. Further thanks are due the Rev. David Preus and Dr. George F. Hall who gave occasion and encouragement. Needless to say, the countless hours of discussion of abstract and concrete issues with students, with colleagues, with teachers and with friends makes one a debtor many times over. Both the University of Minnesota and Yale University have given me more than years of teaching could ever repay.

—PAUL L. HOLMER

[1] Romans X. The translation is J. B. Phillips. *Letters to Young Churches* (New York, 1951), p. 23.

CHAPTER ONE

Learning About the Christian Faith

We are in the midst of what looks like a veritable flood of learning about religious matters. The Christian heritage has been studied with astounding detail since about 1800, particularly in these last few decades. Today our scholars are busy with detailed studies of a host of phenomena related to faith and its survival. Thus, both Old and New Testaments with their historical contexts, their language, their styles, and their ways of meaning have been and are being analyzed with remarkable acumen. Likewise, the practices of the Church, its history, its forms, its relations with other institutions, its many phases and emphases, have also been described and ordered to various intellectual concerns. Even liturgies, sacraments, ceremonies, dogmas, creeds, language, morals, social causes, psychological effects, concepts, Church fathers, and many more facets have been analyzed and summarized for our edification and instruction.

Sometimes this flurry of activity on behalf of religious interests is mistakenly assumed to mean an increase of faith. Our generation is credited falsely with more religion and deeper piety when we ought to be accorded only the slight honor that goes with producing more books and amassing a larger quantity of learning about religion than the world has ever known.

But there is a more serious mistake in all of this, too. Sometimes it is believed that all of this learning about religion is a net gain in theology. Or, to put it another way, sometimes this learning about Christian faith is confused with theology. There is a distinction to be drawn; learning about the things of the faith is not the same as learning to be faithful. But, if that seems too patent, it might be said that theology is the learning of faith, not the learning about faith. Thus the distinction is drawn with the help of two prepositions, of and about. Certainly the use of these two words indicates something rather strong—the fact that the learning and language about religious things are not commensurable with the learning and language of the religious life.[1] This means, in turn, that we have to learn where our learning really belongs. No confusions are so persistent and so involved as those we get into when we get a little learning. This book is an attempt to show what some religious learning is, but also to indicate that confusions do still abound and that they are really avoidable.

It might be said that the amplitude of learning in our day has encouraged the view that there is now a better kind of theology, a new and shiny kind of believing, fit for the "cognoscendi." We hear talk about modern theology, progressive thought, and new kinds of orthodoxy, almost as if all of the language of the Christian man were borrowed from the vocabulary of the learned. Now that there is an easily discerned body of learning about religion, the confusion is correspondingly easy to succumb to. Furthermore, it is the case that larger num-

---

[1] A lengthy treatment of this theme will be found in the pages of the first issue of the journal published by the Society for the Scientific Study of Religion. Note the article by the author and comment by Professor Harmon Holcomb.

bers of people are getting in on this new learning about religion than heretofore, especially with the help of cheap books, college courses, popular lectures and the like. Consequently, the occasions for learning seem to multiply the occasions for sophisticated kinds of confusions.

II

A word of caution must be given, however. For often Christians have sensed the temptation of learning just as they have the temptation of money or affluence, power or authority. The easy resolution has been to suggest that the desire for learning was simply sinful. Not very many thoughtful people have been so candid, but still the anti-intellectual theme has had a kind of quiet authority among Christians. It is never very clear whether the religious anti-intellectual diatribes are caused by a dislike for intellectual work, a downright incapacity, or a serious evaluation of the potential for distraction from God that learning also can be. However, it is one thing to see that the radical difference between a Christian and an unbeliever is not due to a difference in what they know or how much they know, and quite another thing to evaluate the significance of knowing with justice and acumen, subtlety and poise. Part of the successful rendering of the significance of knowledge to ourselves depends upon seeing what knowledge is, what it does for us, how limited it is, what it can not do, and so on.

Any kind of learning satisfies curiosity. This is why even the learning about religion is chiefly a response to our own questions about it. The progress of learning depends upon a talent to ask questions and a myriad of talents to discover their answers. Intellectual curiosity is quite different than a religious interest. And some people may well feel that their religious interests are served by their intellectual efforts. Others may also feel that their religious enthusiasms have been replaced by more mature intellectual concerns. Right here is the source of the confusion.

Pascal, the extraordinary French scientist and man of letters, notes a kind of vanity of the sciences. He says: "La science des choses exterieurs ne me consolera pas de l'ignorance de la morale, au temps d'affliction."[1] Translated this says: "The science of physical things will not, in times of affliction, make up for the lack of moral practice." Pascal, one of the most gifted scientists and mathematicians, over and over again notes what he dares to call the *folly* of science and of philosophy. For men with intellectual curiosity invariably tend to construe the difficulties of living in the world as though they were largely due to human ignorance. Certainly there is no vanity in knowing the truth about something, but there is a deplorable folly in believing that knowledge will solve intimate ethical needs, continuing emotional wants, or even determine our attitudes. One might paraphrase or at least interpret Pascal's devastating remark to fit many intelligentsia:

The easiest conditions to live in according to the world are the most difficult to live in according to God, and vice versa. Nothing is so difficult according to the world as the religious life; nothing is easier than to live it according to God. Nothing is easier, according to the world, than to live in high office and great wealth; nothing is more difficult than to live in them according to God, and without acquiring an interest in them and a liking for them.[2]

Many intelligent people believe that knowing about God and the Bible is going to help them immensely in becoming

---

[1]*Pascal's Pensees.* The edition from which this is quoted is H. F. Stewart's (New York, 1950), whose order is different than other editions of the same aphorisms. This is no. 105, p. 52.

[2]*Pensees.* Translated by T. W. Trotter (New York, Modern Library), no. 905, p. 316.

Christians. Yet we have slight evidence to show that there is more faith just because there is more knowledge—even about Christian matters. What is the easiest condition for the man of learning, or where knowledge abounds, is not necessarily the easiest condition for becoming a Christian.

However, the folly of which Pascal has spoken lies in the mistaken belief that accompanies the learning; it is not in the learning itself. For, the learned man also has his pride, and his pride expresses itself in both bold and subtle ways. The bold manifestation of pride causes the substitution of learning for faith. There are numerous people who practice learning and scholarship at the expense of their faith. They are the people who say that religion belongs to the childhood of the race and that it remains to be replaced by enlightenment and education. Among students of today, it means among other things simply giving up religious ways of thinking, talking and acting in favor of some other ways, simultaneously insisting that modern learning gives reasons against the old and reasons for the new.

Another and more subtle folly is oftentimes practiced by people of the Christian faith. For Christians, too, have doubts about intellectual matters. Major convictions of the tradition are not always easy to assimilate, and reasons for doubting some of them are often discovered in the course of a lifetime. Whether Jesus rose from the dead, whether Mary was the Virgin Mother of our Lord, whether faith is a conditioned response, are typically dubious to many sophisticated persons. For some doubters, matters become increasingly worse; incredulity deepens and is soon entangled with a host of anxieties. Soon the questioning becomes systematic and seems to have no stopping point at all. Doubt becomes general and leads to the somewhat inchoate and ill-defined issues most of us have either entertained or heard others expound. Is there anything at all to religion? Is it only

for infants? Is it all nonsense? Is it only for the stupid and acqui-
escent? In the middle of such inclusive doubting, the young
person either gives up religion altogether or discovers that
there is something called Christian scholarship.

The discovery of scholarship about religion in general and
about Christianity in particular is undoubtedly heartening to
many. After all, it is consoling to know that not everyone has
been unsophisticated and naive on religious matters, but that
there is a number of things to learn and to argue. Right
here is where the folly begins to make a place for itself. Without
being very clear about himself and the issues at stake, the young
learner can easily let the passion for the new life in Christ, the
genuine root of need and quest, be diverted into an enthusiasm
for scholarship about Christ, about Christian ideas, about the
thousand and one things that scholars have uncovered. In brief,
the focus may change, almost imperceptibly, from an interest
in being a Christian to an interest about Christian things.

This folly is easy and deceptive. It comes quietly to most,
almost like an unfolding of their spirits. It seems to climax their
growth and lend spirituality to their intelligence; but it is a folly
nonetheless. Duplicity it remains, however attractive learning
looks decked out in the robes of piety. But, it is only fair to admit
that learning about religion looks very much like religion itself,
and, therefore, the temptation is almost irresistible. Learning
about arithmetic remains arithmetic, and learning about geography is geography; but learning about morals is not the same
as being moral, and learning about faith is not necessarily being
faithful.

Therefore, it is incumbent upon the reader to recognize the
dangers in caressing the world's scholarship about Jesus Christ,
the Bible, and the many things associated with the faith. Admittedly, these dangers are not imminent for very many. In fact,

on the contrary, most people do not suffer from too much reflection. Still, it is a needful reminder for the student, who slides so smoothly from an early passion for Christian things, a consuming concern about himself and his relation to God, to a secondhand acquaintance. This is often how it is. A person begins with a firsthand and immediate need and ends with a secondhand and mediated resolution. One of the easiest achievements is a kind of chatty consciousness of what scholars have said. Despite the respectability of this kind of resolution of religious concern, still it is a folly, if not a gross error, for the human spirit to let that substitute for a firsthand Christian life and its appropriate assurances.

Such dangers exist chiefly for the learned. In ages past, as Pascal noted in the quotation already cited, high office and great wealth were the universal goals. Few people, however, succeeded in synthesizing prominence and a humbling faith, Mammon and God. So, Pascal certainly made a justifiable point in noting the difficulty of living with them and according to God. High office and great wealth are still widely sought and esteemed as great goods, but now something else has been added to the range of possibilities. In our day of affluence, learning is not only the means to office and wealth, but it is also self-empowering. It seems to be personally efficacious; besides it is cheap. If you can not be distinguished or wealthy, you still can be learned or half-learned. The lore of the ages is easier to acquire today than ever before in history. For many gifted people, those with strong drives towards knowledge and continuing curiosities, the world becomes increasingly bearable when they know about it. With curiosities thwarted and ignorance rife, the world is an intolerable chaos, opaque to forethought and plan. With knowledge, a little order begins to appear; and the promise of knowledge is that the order will increase in extent and detail.

The abundance of riches, our Lord made clear, was a somewhat dubious condition for getting into heaven. The camel straining to get through the needle's eye is the image to suggest the rich man's plight. It is not so easy to speak conclusively and fulsomely about learning. For one thing, the Christian churches have been associated with the life of learning almost since the day of their inception. Learning has been a vehicle of faith, almost the crucible of its passions and the criterion for its expressions. But learning can also be an invasion, almost another mask, by which the major issues are averted or postponed. More than this, learning can, as the Apostle Paul suggested, puff a man up to amazing proportions. And now the puffing up goes on in the name of faith and religious progress; for almost everyone finds the obligation to learn about the faith to be more essential than being faithful.

These remarks make sense only if there is a distinction to be drawn between the learning *about* religion, on the one hand, and the learning *of* religion, on the other. Stated less ambiguously there is a language *of* one's faith and a language *about* things religious. The creation of scholarly disciplines designed to study religious materials is a very great achievement of the human spirit. It cannot be eschewed; but this language and literature is not theology proper. Theology is a language and learning expressive of pathos, enthusiasm, and even passion. When passion is qualified properly by Jesus Christ, then men are certainly on the road to being Christians. Theology has its genesis among those who have a powerful faith in Jesus Christ and who begin to refer all things in heaven and on earth to God. Theologians try to speak truly. They make judgments, they evaluate, they characterize, they rhapsodize, they sing, and they even argue with adversaries.

The crucial matter to keep in mind is that the language of

faith is not actually the fruit of technical scholarship. It is not a language about faith at all. But there is a language about faith which is available for all who can learn it. It ought to be clear that scientific and scholarly accounts of anything, including religious ideas—the mind of Paul, the teachings of Jesus, the faith of Peter, the creed of the Apostles—all such accounts must be disinterested and detached in order to succeed as descriptions of the phenomena in question. The increase of this kind of religious learning has caused many people to believe that all of this learning about Christianity is theology itself; but this is not true. Theology is the language of Christian enthusiasm; and it is not detached and disinterested. On the contrary, the language of Luther, of Augustine, of Paul, of Calvin, is rich in pathos, discerning in judgment, strict in evaluation, and dominated invariably by distinctively Christian categories. Religious scholarship progresses through the years, and usually the later is better than the earlier. But it is not clear that theology progresses in the same way. This is why confessional documents of the sixteenth century are still meaningful to Christians of the twentieth century; this is why Augustine's theology is still so widely read by so many people, whereas his views on most historical and scientific matters—magnetism, for example—are only curiosities.

Perhaps this is but another reminder of the fact that being perfected in faith and being perfected in knowledge are two quite distinct characteristics. No one can deny that being perfected in both is desirable. It is also true that an intimate command of a vast array of knowledge about Christian literature and history is compatible with a command of pathos in the Christian manner. Apparently, neither kind of command is easy by itself; and putting them together is unlikely but not impossible.

III

However, confusions between these two kinds of religious speech are very old. One must remember that disciplines about a variety of things, i.e., sciences and systematic studies, are really rather new. Though certain kinds of objective studies and disinterested explanations of various phenomena have been proposed since very early times, it is only within the past few centuries that we have had widespread research and learning. Earlier general explanations, usually of a very general philosophic or theologic kind, did service for all kinds of explanation. One might put the matter this way—that the rise of a learning about religious matters is one more item in the history of objective study and explanation. Objective learning in the *about* temper is a slow accumulation, and religious learning in this genre is one of the most recent in that process.

Christians have had to learn to live with the language about religious matters, just as they have had to learn to live with the new language, i.e., the scientific language, about the natural world. The presence of the new and scientific kind of explanations and the optimisms that accompanied their rise among us led some people to a somewhat odd and unfortunate point of view. The older and different ways of talking and of explaining, genetic, historical, teleological, and even theological were considered outmoded, and it was frequently said that they were to be replaced by positive sciences. Persons of a scientific bent found great difficulty in accepting the notion that there were a diverse number of ways of construing the world. But religious people also found it difficult to add the more mechanical and causal ways of talking to their vocabulary too. For those accustomed to the language of the Bible and theological explanation, the rise of scientific learning has meant that they must learn the difference between scientific accounts and theological accounts. The two ways are not really commensurable; and both can be learned and talked without contradiction or inconsistency.[3]

Certainly there are many difficulties for religious people here. For one thing, there is the fact that theological ways of talking about the world are much older, and all kinds of alien factors have accrued to theology in the passage of time. Theology has been taught to many persons as though it were the exclusive and only truthful way of speaking. Also, theological ways of talking are taught us very early in life, and consequently such ways of speaking and reflecting become associated with a wide variety of precious associations, not all of them adding to the flexibility of belief and understanding.

The rise of learning about religion has both helped and hindered the cause of faith among us. This is the way one would suspect matters to be simply from the neutral character of learning itself. The extraordinary achievements in historical study, in psychological analysis, in Biblical criticism and the rest which we will be subsequently noting, demand both the effort to assimilate this modern reflection within our religious thought and our theology, and also a kind of challenge to a Christian consciousness to make good its claims. That there must be modifications in knowledge, continuous and even radical, is by now an old story and is told by the very history of every branch of knowledge. Whether the modifications in theology have been or ought to be so grand is another matter altogether. In some of the chapters which will follow, it will be seen that changes in theology are really rather slight, despite the trumpeting that has gone on.

If one reads the Augsburg Confession, widely ascribed to by

---

[3]Note in this regard Volume One in this Lutheran Studies Series. It is A. van der Ziel's *The Natural Sciences and the Christian Message* (T. S. Denison and Co., 1960).

Lutheran churches the world over, one discovers an attempt to bring together the principal Christian theological teachings. This very brief document of some twenty-eight articles was written by Philip Melanchthon in 1530 for the use of those minor princes and free cities who had to make a case for their dissenting views discussed at the Diet of Augsburg. Charles V was intent upon defending his empire against the Turks and against the ever threatening dissensions arising from within. The Christian religion no longer bound the empire into one. The thought of "une foi, un roi, une loi" gave great promise to Charles as it had to earlier Frenchmen.

The Augsburg Confession is a statement of what the princes and their pastors taught and believed. In a sense, it is a summary of their knowledge of God. The claim of Melanchthon and Luther, as of so many others in the history of religious controversy, was that the new teaching as thus summarized was in accord with Scripture. Furthermore, they contended that it was in accord with the Fathers of the early Church and the central traditions of the Catholic Church.

In brief, it might be said that such a confession (like those coming out of Scotland, Holland, and England) tends to point its hearer and reader to the Holy Scripture. In a day when Melanchthon could write rather confidently that "the world is aging, man's nature is gradually growing weaker . . ."[1] it was perhaps easier to point to the past anyway. Even without a profound respect for the Scripture as the very word of God, many men referred their doubts to the past on the ground that the earlier was plainly better than the later. However, in Christian circles, the Scriptures, and especially the New Testament, have had another and peculiar claim. The Holy Writ always has seemed to be the only source in which the distinct and completely different characteristics of the Chosen People and of

[1]*Augsburg Confession* (St. Louis, n.d.), Article XXIII, p. 29.

Jesus of Nazareth were made clear. Thus, if anyone doubted, if anyone confessed to not understanding what was being declared, both Jews and Christians have for a long while pointed the doubter to the Bible.

Once the teaching of the Church did a double service. It provided for many, as Galileo critically noted, both the knowledge of how to move into heaven and how the heavens moved. Perhaps theology claimed too much. It is also true that Melanchthon in the Confession and many other careful theologians of Christian history were very painstaking about theology, and they have tried to keep it directed to the salvation of men and not allow it to masquerade as exhaustive explanations of everything in the world. Part of the glory of recent scholarship in historical theology and in Biblical matters is the account which corrects an exaggerated view long current in semi-sophisticated circles. However, in the absence of knowledge such as we have, knowledge of the Reformation, of the Bible's contents, one must admit that it was easy to use the Scripture as the point of departure for many kinds of views, not only theological evaluation, but about all kinds of matters.

It does not seem that church confessions have suffered very much with the passage of time. They have the kind of durability that Scripture itself does, probably because they are so close in content to that originating source. Churches continue to use theology in confessional form because such confessions state briefly the content of what is believed and because the Bible's Gospel is manifested in them more clearly than it is in more extended documents. Creeds are of the same quality. Perhaps they, too, were conceived to help defend the Bible's message, to get at the minimum essentials and to make public the bonds of conviction between people who believed they were called of God.

Furthermore, it must be admitted that churches are not very good at making up new confessions anyway. Theology does not grow easily through church conventions and synodical documents. The kind of theology we see thriving today is historically oriented once again. Much of it comes about in virtue of a rediscovery of what the Reformers are saying. This has come about in a variety of ways. In part it reflects a closer and an unprejudiced reading of historical sources. Biblical and historical scholars have made the literature of the past clearer to us. Confusions of learning that made us read these things as if their authors were myth-makers, bad metaphysicians and divine soothsayers have been disspelled. The spread of learning has not uniformly destroyed our respect for convictions of the past as we were taught to expect. As learning has moved over new territories, for example, the human mind, natural phenomena, the structure of society and historical phenomena hitherto unknown, religious men have not seen everything within theology destroyed.

In fact, it is almost as if the learning of the world has created both confusions and clarity for the Christians. Some things have had to be restated, but some things now look good again. The Bible looms large once again. And because this is true, the church confessions and time-honored creeds, which reflect the Scripture so clearly also come in for a new respect. Again we must say that the extent of learning, its manysidedness and detail, has let us practice a kind of neutrality and objectivity wherein some views were seen to be not a part of Christian teaching and others were. Such a winnowing, though it is painful to each of us, is part of the life of the mind. Again it is clear that faith is not intellectually earned, even for those who can think, anymore than it was morally earned in the time of the Apostles, centuries ago.

These venerated documents of religious faith, creeds, Bible, and confessions, are really the chief means in our language to get the consciousness of men adequately defined in a Christian manner. It is unfortunate that many other views have entered in, that mistaken judgments about natural phenomena were included, that convictions about a flat world and celestial spheres were believed to be Christian. But the purposes of scholarship about the faith is not to create the faith or even a new theology, for scholarship does not engender theology nor does it represent the latest and most probable account of God's presence and action. The upshot is quite different. Scholarship has given people freedom, not to create new creeds and new faiths, for this they have always had, but rather to see what theology actually is when everything else has been stripped away.

IV

One of the greatest philosophers of modern times, Immanuel Kant, remarked rather casually that he had destroyed knowledge in order to make room for faith. His judgment is not the expression of a misologist, a man who hates to think, but is, rather, a thoughtful conviction by one of the greatest of intellectual masters. Kant discovered that ethical and religious commitments were invariably tangled up with knowledge claims of various sorts. At least many ethical and religious leaders in Kant's day, as in ours, talk as if a commitment to an ethical responsibility or faith in the triune God were a matter of knowledge first and action secondarily.

Kant called this kind of dependence an instance of heteronomy, by which he meant that religion and moral action were conceived to be subject to laws or principles external to themselves. Another way to describe heteronomy would be to say that knowledge was conceived to have many functions besides teaching something, including that of producing ethical action and religious faith. Kant's plea instead was for the autonomy of ethicality and faith. Literally he argued that the "nomos," the law or principle of moral behavior, was not derived from something else, nor was faith a consequence of knowledge.

Kant's views have been persuasive for large numbers of people ever since. No one is arguing here that he is right or wrong. However, what he said about the autonomy of faith and morals has become pertinent to a large segment of modern learning. With the neutralization of learning, which has gone on during the past two centuries, all kinds of scholars have, like Kant, said that knowledge does not produce faith. Neither does it destroy it as so many practitioners of the intellectual life used to say. As knowledge becomes more precisely ordered, the learned have to admit not only their ignorance but also that there is plenty of room left for faith and for theology. In fact, those who have closed all the doors and said that knowledge would destroy faith are wrong.

This is evident in the scientific study of religious phenomena. Today we witness an odd kind of backwash. The optimism of the learned minority, who promised that more learning would really produce a new faith and modern theologies, is fairly well dissipated. We are beginning to see that contemporary learning has little to contribute directly to a theological view; for theological convictions are not hypotheses, and they are not probable or improbable on the basis of evidence. The passing of time and the accumulation of learning has little to augment them or to alter them fundamentally. Therefore, we witness in our day a new heartiness among many learned people, a willingness to address themselves to theological and moral convictions in a firsthand and immediate way, without the debilitating and enervating thought that only scholarship can prepare the way.

This is in part what is meant by the theological revival in our time. Once again the learned have an open sesame to faith; and religion, not least the Christian faith, seems an open possibility. More than this is the fact that the older theologies of the early church and of the Reformation are now blessed with a kind of contemporaneity that makes them real options. This is an incidental fruit of scientific scholarship. Confusions still abound, but in the pages which follow, a few topics will be explored by which clarity enters too.

CHAPTER TWO

Psychoanalysis and Faith: Erich Fromm

No one can pretend to finality on the question of the compatibility of psychoanalysis and religion, and least of all the author, who is only a professor. For one thing, the question is not as clear as one might wish. There are undoubtedly many persons who are religious and who have been psychoanalyzed, and with some of these persons it makes sense to say that analysis did not dissipate their religion. On the other hand, there may be people who are *neurotically* religious, who, when they command their neuroses in some fashion, or let us say it more charitably, when they are no longer behaving neurotically, no longer behave religiously. If this is true, one may be saying nothing more than that being neurotic and religious simultaneously is difficult, and knowing about one's neuroses and being religious is even more difficult. On the level of behavior, in other words, there seem to be people who stay religious when analyzed; and there are analysts who are religious and religious people who become analysts.

But there are areas about which it is not easy to speak with assurance. What religious people say about certain phenomena does seem to contradict what psychoanalysts sometimes say about the same phenomena. And then the strain is not in the same area at all. Instead of asking whether one can be religious and analyzed, the issue is whether both sets of claims about human nature can be true. When Freud said religion had a future, even though religion was illusory, he surely was saying something quite different from, and logically contradictory to, that said by most of the pious. All the razzle-dazzle one might introduce on the importance and even the necessity of illusions does not mitigate for the religious or for Freud the difference between religion being claimed to be true about God and man and psychoanalysis being said to be true about the illusion concerning God and man. In this latter instance, there is an incompatibility between the assertions found within much of psychoanalytic literature, on the one hand, and religious literature on the other, and this is because they predicate diversely and even contradictorily about the same things.

It is not being urged that this is the impasse upon which the human race is hung. I suspect that there is no definitive either—or available at the moment. Neither the psychoanalysts, who have spoken so opportunely, nor the religious, who have countered so vociferously, are entirely right about each other. In fact, there is an embarrassing plentitude of books written by religious authors in our day, who tell us that Freud was wrong in the metaphysics (where heaven knows it is difficult to be anything else) but right in his human dynamics, his psychotherapeutics. Not to be outdone, the analysts are writing books and articles too, beating their breasts in public, to show that their story was a little premature, that it is not quite so clear as some of the early apostles of cultural sanity had said. There has been a blurring of the lines, a softening of the cries of victory, a tendency to repudiate the monolithic urge that early analysis encouraged.

There have been several confusions on these matters. Sometimes people of intellectual bent have overgeneralized and overextended their views. It is a readily understood temptation to want to extend every hypothesis about a limited subject matter to other troublesome areas of widespread concern. For example, there do not seem to be scientific answers to most ethical problems, to political issues, to religious difficulties. Psychoanalysts who, like the psychologists of all time, have studied human behavior and its causes, have not always resisted this great temptation. They have frequently pontificated about matters where they should properly have been journeymen researchers instead.

The cry for increasing objectivity among men of learning is not a fortuitous and accidental phenomenon. For objectivity is precisely that human temper which anyone needs who says only what he knows, who must limit himself to what the evidence permits and suggests. Surely one of the reasons for the circumspection of modern psychoanalysis, and contemporary psychology of other kinds too, is that there has been a widespread recognition of the need for more objectivity and, correspondingly, for less easy and enthusiastic talk about numerous difficult matters.

Sometimes this kind of objectivity is misunderstood. It is contended that scientists and scholars are refusing to take their responsibilities seriously when they do not talk generously and quasi-scientifically about everything of human concern. Part of the progress of science is simply a matter of learning how to speak precisely and circumspectly about a very limited subject matter. Many people misunderstand those who study human behavior on this very count. They want on scientific grounds what science can not provide. They want moral judgments, wide generalizations, immediately useful policies—anything but scientific explanations and exact descriptions. What appears to be a weakness—the reluctance to speak on germanely human issues—may be a strength, especially if it is occasioned by an awareness of the limits of one's knowledge. Furthermore, this kind of progress in scientific study augurs well for both moral judgments and theological generalizations; for it means very probably that we are learning not to moralize or to theologize on irrelevant grounds.

But psychologists and psychoanalysts are also human beings. Most of them also have moral, religious, and a host of other interests. Erich Fromm among the psychoanalysts is one of the most catholic. While he is to be admired for getting a hearing, he also has to be read with care; for he tends to use psychological generalizations for his springboard into all kinds of fascinating realms. Certainly he knows his moments of restraint, but his moments of boundless enthusiasm are more frequent. He is almost a preacher, a homiletician, for psychoanalysis. He keeps up that odd practice, reminiscent of Freud himself, of enlarging psychoanalytic judgments to include everything human, all the while as if a new learning were on his side. He essays the largest issues, nothing less than ethics in *Man for Himself,* myth and rituals in *The Forgotten Language,* the body politic in *The Sane Society,* and then religion in *Psychoanalysis and Religion.* These latter pages were the Terry Lectures at Yale and are published by the press of that university.

Mr. Fromm's discussions of religious matters are certainly in the genre previously noted. They are about religion and about religious behavior. But the author does not draw a distinction between language *about* religion and the language *of* religion. Instead, his pages abound in a kind of theologizing, but it turns out that psychoanalytic language about human behavior leads him smoothly and without strain right into a language of advocacy, of enthusiasm and of a kind of ethical, if not religious, pathos.

Mr. Fromm speaks for neither psychological nor religious orthodoxies. Maybe he is neither psychologically effective nor religiously edifying; but it does seem clear that his pages force reflection. Indirectly they seem to me to push the Christian theologian's definitions quite a little. We will turn, therefore, to several of his provocative themes.

II

An overarching theme throughout his book on religion is the provocatively stated one that what matters for psychoanalysts and priests (this is Fromm's generic name, I take it, for priests, ministers, pastors, rabbis) is whether a person "lives love and thinks truth." Few of us can deny that conduct is very important, that behavior is often a better test of what we are than our words, so certainly the initial thrust of his words can not be disregarded. Mr. Fromm goes on to suggest something that is rather popular—that the matter of living *love* and thinking *truth* is more important than the symbol systems we use to talk about ourselves. This is one way in which the author denigrates theology, by suggesting that its words are often idle and that another way is available to test human adequacy.

It is almost as if the languages of morals and of religion are, therefore, the wrong place to have one's concern. These "symbolic systems," for this is what Fromm calls them, have often been made matters of subscription. Fromm thinks this is a mistake. Psychological study now shows why this is a mistake. Furthermore, the language of everyday usage, like the language of morals and of religion, has made us believe that the world is different than it actually is.

The facts are dreadful enough. Man cannot afford to live, as social conditions now are, in a loving manner. Neither can he know and tell the truth about himself and others. The world is made for hating and lying. The language systems, philosophies and theologies, depict the world as if it were otherwise. The upshot is that men become sick unto death. They yield to the world and its ways, albeit retaining the capacity to judge themselves as wanting and to suffer the hurt that comes from knowing something so unpleasant. They accept for true what the majority wants to be true, they rationalize irrational passions, they orient their lives to the herd while striving to be individuals. This is what Fromm describes as a dichotomous situation. Whites hate Negroes, Gentiles hate Jews, Americans hate Russians. The hating is for socially acceptable reasons. Meanwhile, amid the hate, the competition, the will to win, men also wish to be loving, kind, tolerant, democratic, Christian, and moral. Most of this is only talk; they espouse loving kindness, yet find little in their environment strengthening that resolution. Likewise, they reason, they command criteria for the truth, they judge, they criticize, they consult evidence, they measure the relativities involved. Again, however, there are compulsive and generating factors in society which turn them to another kind of *truth,* that which is said to be *truth* because it is easy, in accord with authority, the best for everyone, expressive of the spirit of the time, the modern and accepted way of thinking about matters.

Fromm wants us to believe that "living love and thinking truth" is the *sine qua non* of being human, and furthermore, that psychoanalysts have discovered this much. Psychoanalysts, he says repeatedly, have found that giving in to the dichotomous resolution means an unproductive, noncreative personality. Anyone who fails to achieve maturity and integration, in fact develops a neurosis of one kind or another. And a neurosis, at least as Fromm describes it, means that a person cannot love others; he thinks to his own intellectual detriment; he creates pictures which are illusory and clings to them with a tenacity which is incommensurate with their supposed quality. Perhaps it is a phenomenon like one of the Chicago newspapers having to tell you on its masthead that it is the world's greatest newspaper—which, if it were true, would not have to be reiterated in every issue.

Up to this point Fromm sounds almost like a Christian theologian. One cannot help but wonder where he got this view that men had to live love and think truth in order to be human. He says that for him it stems from psychoanalytic practice and theory, and, of course, he may be right. But it seems to have had a longer history. Furthermore, there is a little difficulty in showing that a command saying that a man ought to be loving and ought to be truthful ever follows from any kind of fact whatsoever. Dr. Fromm is not very specific on this matter and perhaps he does not feel he has to be as long as he is so clearly, on this point at least, on the side of the angels.

But there is another theme, and this is in answer to the question, What is religion? "Any system of thought and action shared by a group which gives the individual a frame of orientation and an object of devotion," is a religion. I am not concerned with the question of whether this makes any sense or not. Granting this definition, there is a great deal of religion in the world. When you begin thinking about the thoughts and actions, the suggestions, the admonitions, the projects, the vocations, the political creeds, the common-sense convictions around which major industries and institutions grow up, then you get a clue to what Fromm is willing to call religion. "Frames of orientation and objects of devotion"—they are after all *plural,* and there is a kind of competition for souls. To an individual this may mean dichotomous or trichotomous frames and/or objects of devotion. Seen from another vantage point, everyone has a kind of religious need, i.e., a need for a frame of orientation and an object of devotion. This assertion, too, is straight from the analyst's mouth. Men may get their orientation and devotion with and by visible gods, saints, ancestors, nations, classes, money, or cleanliness. There is, therefore, a wide swath cut in human societies which is, according to Fromm, religious.

Another major discovery of the psychoanalysts is that, therefore, no one can be without a religion. It was a mistake of the earlier psychologists and psychoanalysts to say otherwise. The issue is instead which kind of religion—one which furthers man's development or one which paralyzes him? Despite the warnings of other students of these matters, William James and numerous others, Fromm contends that the psychological analysts along with the religious leaders are interested in the *value* of religions, not only in their causes or what he calls their "psychological roots." Defending the thesis that "the need for a frame of orientation and an object of devotion is rooted in the conditions of man's existence," Fromm says the issue is really how the need is going to be satisfied. In this perspective every neurosis looks like a *private* form of religion, an inadequate religion because the individual is badly oriented and badly devoted.

III

Now surely, saying this much is to skip a lot of difficulties. It means that precision and exactness have been forsaken. Anyone can say easily enough, "What does Fromm mean by 'badly oriented'?" How does he know? But now the first theme returns. "Badly oriented" means that a man does not live love and think truth. There are countless religions because there are countless frames of orientation and objects of devotion. But the point to which we have been brought by Mr. Fromm's argument is that the analysts, a kind of blessed tribe at least if they are right, now are able to tell us that "living love and thinking truth" is the necessary and universal condition for being human, for productivity, and for the good life.

Whether every detail is correct or not, there is surely something important in all of this. It seems that Fromm has discovered, or at least he believes he has discovered, what Christian faith has always said:—that everyone must choose this day whom he shall serve. This is commonplace enough but never trivial. On the contrary, it is most important. This fact about people, that they need orientation and an object of devotion, enables Fromm to get to religious matters from other concerns. Paul Tillich, among the Christian theologians, also exploits this fact and uses it to characterize human existence. What he calls the science of ontology is precisely the science of what it means for anything to be. According to Tillich, to be human requires the exercise of decision and choice and distinguishes the "being" of persons from the being of everything else. The interest of Tillich and many existentialist theologians has been quickened by just such themes as Fromm has developed.

But there is still another matter to note: analytic therapy is essentially an attempt to help the patient gain or regain his capacity for love. This is the psychoanalyst's medicine for the soul and an area of overlap with religion, not all of it to be sure, but some of it. Religion with a capital "R," organized, institutional religion is, as Mr. Fromm sees it, usually authoritarian. It demands belief, obedience, and worship of the God it declares. Authoritarian religion is incompatible, Fromm thinks, with the analyst's discoveries and surely with what he, Fromm, has been saying. The kind of religion which is *humanistic,* self-developmental, which specializes in creativity, in a richer and better humanity, in the unfolding of a person's powers of love and reason—this kind is not threatened by psychoanalysis. On the contrary, this kind of religion finds that psychoanalysis contributes a great deal to its realization.

At this juncture it is clear that Mr. Fromm is playing the pontiff for the human race. He finds that the see of St. Sigmund (Freud, that is) still permits him the luxurious privilege of declaring the faith to all men. Even if it is not the faith once-for-all delivered to the saints, it is still a faith—modern, psychoanalytically approved — and full of promise for the race. Furthermore, it condones the joint efforts of priests and psychotherapists. Fromm is mightily persuaded by all of this and touchingly persuasive besides. One could have hoped, however, that a little more scrutiny be given such persuasiveness before it became a book. For what facts open to the psychologists command this proposal? What views of even authoritarian religion finally exclude what Fromm and most men agree is so desirable? This is a matter for the reflection of each reader and a reminder that an author cannot do everything for the reader.

After all of this has been read, the new harmony proposed and a certain obviousness made even more obvious, one might be inclined to ask, "What in thunder is all the fuss about?" Mr. Fromm is for truth, beauty, goodness, love, and reason. Who is not? But the irony of Mr. Fromm's whole treatment of the difficulties between psychoanalysis and religion is that he can resolve the differences only by proposing *another* religion, one which includes psychoanalysis and the proper frame of orientation and object of devotion. One is reminded of the gentleman who was asked to walk the chalked line in the police station to prove his sobriety. He did it, but betrayed his drunkenness by the extraordinary effort it took him to do it.

CHAPTER THREE

Historical Research and Faith

The title of this chapter suggests a perennial issue for religious people who reflect. Is faith a consequent to historical research? Is religiousness somehow established and/or disestablished by archeology, by analysis of texts, by confirmation of hypotheses about historical events and peoples?

This may seem a trivial question and obvious enough to answer. But the difficulty is that the "obviousness" is a duplex phenomenon. It seems equally obvious to some persons that historical research is a way to establish or disestablish faith and to others that nothing is so clearly irrelevant to religiousness as historical research.

It must be clear to everyone concerned that there are some religions which are not affected at all by any kind of recognition of past events or persons. I believe most Buddhists and many Hindus, probably many Confucianists, do not care a whit about the religious implications of historical research. They need not care because their religion in no way depends upon claims about past events or past personages. And if their god or their gods stand related in any way to human events, that relation is described in ethical commands and is couched, perhaps, in language both psychological and admonitory, which is suggestive of conduct. The validity of the commands, for example in Buddhism, does not depend upon their historical genesis at all; instead their validity is claimed to be an intrinsic quality, soliciting the immediate approval of the would-be believer.

In some religions, which, in an important sense, are non-historical, no problem arises concerning the historicity of events or persons. Or rather one might say that if the problem arises, it is only for the superstitiously religious, and they are those who have tied the authority of an ethic to a supposed miraculous and extra-natural origin. The point made by sophisticated Buddhists and Hindus is that the apprehension of the intrinsically religious, the way of life, is not dependent upon the apprehension of anything else. What there is to be apprehended is self-certifying, self-authenticating, and needs no alien authoritative and quasi-historical source.

Clearly the religions of the Islamic people, of Jews, and of Christians are quite different. These religions are intimately tied to historical events. Even the laws of Judaism, which are admonitory and obliging and can be entertained in separation from their origin and history, do not make their practitioners Jews. The matter is not that simple. The Jews are an historical community of long standing, of well-defined character, and their faith or religiousness is not only law-obedience, but is also tied up, in ways difficult to state simply, with a conviction about the relationship between that community and a living and historically interested God. He is the God of Abraham and of Isaac, of history and of persons, of events and of strategies. So, too, is it with the Christians. They claim an historical point of departure — the person of Jesus, who is reputed to have lived and died, to have risen from the dead. One cannot be long concerned about Christianity without also being concerned about the historicity of Jesus. Here, too, one cannot separate Jesus' teachings from His historicity and claim that the teachings have sufficient intrinsic ethical qualities, the recognition and adherence of which is the making of one's faith. The point is that even if the ethics of Judaism or of Jesus Christ or of Mohammed have an immediate significance, which can be enjoined without any further recognition, still very few students of these religions would be willing to say that this immediacy makes men Christians, Jews, or Mohammedans.

All of these latter religions are historical, and every textbook about religion says this over and over. At least one thing meant by saying this is that a necessary condition for being religious in the form suggested (in contrast to Buddhism and Hinduism, for example) is that some convictions about the relationship between God and history must enter into and become a part of the religiousness of Christians, Jews, and Mohammedans. This is why these western religious groups have some kind of stake in "history," most often the kind which says that instead of the religious ethic being self-authenticating and intrinsically efficacious, the ethic is binding because God commanded it, or because a man who was God said it. But be that as it may, it is clear enough that many kinds of historical connection have been claimed and are claimed, and that a belief about these connections between God and men constitute, in part, religious faith.

A fundamental difference is apparent between typically Eastern religions and those of the West. Theologians of Christianity and Judaism have been extremely skeptical of those efforts at synthesizing the world religions or of even the milder insistences to the effect that the essence of all religions is the same. Christian theologians fought this battle in the first centuries of the Church and especially against those called Gnostics. The latter group tried to rid Christianity of many elements which because they were historical were also thought to be non-spiritual and non-ethereal. Some early Gnostics liked to emphasize the spiritual side of everything and believed the wedding of the carnal (and carnal really means fleshly and historical too) and the spiritual in the person of Jesus and the history of the Church was positively vulgar.

The recent interest on the part of many Western writers, Aldous Huxley, Christopher Isherwood, and others, in Buddhism and Hinduism is, in part at least, a protest against this historicizing of religion, this locating of the religious object of affection and adoration in such loci as human flesh, historical communities, and even printed pages. For one thing, to claim an historical genesis and root means that one must be very sure the historical events and personages really happened and lived. Thus the utterly vexatious question of historical proof arises. If one is a Buddhist, there is no need to ask whether Buddha really lived. But a Jew must care about the early community of Jews and their history because his religion demands identifying himself with that community and becoming flesh with their flesh, bone with their bone, blood with their blood. So, too, with the Christians and the historical Jesus.

During the nineteenth century several attempts were made to turn the historical side of the Christian and Jewish religions into something else. This was tempting then because all kinds of severe questions were being raised about the historical accuracy of the Biblical documents and other pieces of ancient literature. The theory of evolution, too, gave some people concern about certain historical claims concerning the origin and early history of man. But somehow the roles of Christianity and Judaism were not dissipated as so many suggested, and many of the historical claims were subsequently reiterated, a little more guardedly but nonetheless reiterated.

But fundamental issues are never really dead. We have still to ask what kinds of things an historian can really know. Most recently these questions have been raised formally—almost abstractly. Historians have wondered with some of the theologians whether historical evidence enables us to say that God watches over Israel, that He neither slumbers nor does He sleep. Does historical evidence really tell us that Jesus was divine, that the Church is a God-created institution?

Are the claims of religion to being historical the kind that historians describe? Are they, even if defined as historical, open to the kind of research that historians have done and are doing? Another way to say this is as follows: suppose one admits the peculiar historical-like relations existing between God and men, which Christianity and Judaism claim. Are those relations open to the processes of historical verification? Some persons answer too quickly. They say that you cannot mean by "historical" something which historians cannot verify. If this is so, then the right to talk about historical claims depends upon the ability of making the supposed claims amenable to research techniques. Others will say, more directly of course, that these matters are historical, and an undue strain and stress will be made to interpret and construe historical events as if they had a patent religious meaning.

Historical research has sometimes become, therefore, the attack upon or the defense of faith. I believe this has made for an untold amount of nonsense, some of it religious nonsense, some of it irreligious nonsense. Persons have been too quick to leap into the breach, to package up the data in religious and/or non-religious forms. Everyone likes to extend one kind of hypotheses to other kinds of areas. All of us have to temper our enthusiasms, to modify our wanton dispositions, so that we do not make hypotheses relevant to one area, explanatory of everything at once.

II

Another way to assess these matters is to focus our attention again upon just what it is that historical assertions do for us. None can doubt that our historical consciousness has been immensely enriched by the variety of studies now available. We know immeasurably more about origins, about sequences, about persons, about causes, about a host of happenings in the past. But this clarification of historical consciousness is still not an immediate religious gain. For such knowledge as we can gather about historical events does not materially change or determine our religious evaluation and judgment of those events.

The Western religions all have their origins around some historical personages and events. Christians believe in Jesus Christ and they believe that He lived and died. Even Christian worship brings the believer back again and again to crucial events in the life history of Jesus Christ. Thus it is that historical language is ingredient in the tissue of most Western religious teaching. But the fact that such language and such claims as are made in that language are essential, does not argue that more historical research is going to mean more theology. The discontinuity between historical language about an event or person and theological language is still large. The amount, whether large or small, of historical language has nothing to do with the theological affirmations.

This point seems confusing to many scholars. The insistence upon historical revelation, that Judaism and Christianity are historical, suggests that there is a dependence of a logical sort of theological statements upon historical statements. This is not the case. The matter can be put in another way, although somewhat technical.

It turns out that theological language, like most forms of speech, contains terms, concepts, propositions, etc. It is not appropriate at the moment to specify each; but concepts do deserve a little attention here. We mean by a concept simply a meaning complex which refers but does not assert. A concept is usually signified by relatively simple linguistic devices— words, for example, rather than sentences or paragraphs. When we speak of a concept, we speak of that way of meaning which does not do much but refer us to something. Words and the way we use words have to be considered. It turns out that Christian theology is full of concepts. Part of the trick of thinking well is to get the "conceptual meaning" of the terms straight and to keep the meaning or meanings straight. The word, "God," in Jewish and Christian usage has a specific meaning. Not everyone who uses the word "God" uses it with such meaning. It is no secret to note that Jews and Christians have a way of getting persons acquainted with that meaning. They do this by telling stories of the exodus of Jews from Egypt, by stories of David, by Psalms and prophetic pieces. And Christians continue the story or stories. They make it plain that the word "God" is also properly used to refer to Jesus of Nazareth, whose life story is known in part.

A concept can, of course, refer to something non-historical. We have concepts of ghosts, of elves, of monsters, and we even can name them if we so choose. We can use language to give social status to imagined beings, ideal creatures and creations, and, thereafter, our concepts can refer to these. There are many concepts of God, some of which seem to be social inventions, contrived for a variety of purposes. Immanuel Kant pointed out that "God" meant a regulative idea, a kind of controlling purpose, for some people. In this instance, the reference of the term was not historical at all. But the Christian and the western way of using the term is certainly to use it to refer to historical events and personages.

The point, then, is that the Judaic-Christian usage of the term "God" is always to be learned in some historical accounts. "God" becomes a concept; and that means only that when the term is used a complex of historical events is the context for the answer. The logician's way of describing this is to say that the concept, a meaning complex, refers to something. But a meaning complex ought not to cause any distress, for all that is meant by that is the peculiar kind of recognition that comes when we say: "Oh, you mean that; now I understand!" Again, in the context of religious faith, the way to make that happen is to tell the stories of the Old Testament and the New.

It is in this sense that theologians have insisted that revelation is historical. One does not learn about God the way he does mathematics. Even the concepts are different. It would be patently absurd to try to get in on the meanings of concepts of geometry and arithmetic in the same way as one does in religion. Therefore, mathematicians do not spend much time on historical study and seem serenely untroubled with its consequences. But in religious affairs, historical research seems always close to the heart of the matter; and countless people talk as if their love for God depended in some odd way upon historical authenticity. All kinds of troubles seem rooted here, troubles about who wrote what, whether Moses ever lived, whether Jesus was mistaken about anything, whether the Bible was inspired.

The crux of the matter might be seen in another way. For even though the term "God" refers to an historical person, at least in the Christian context, still it is not the case that the historical language about Jesus is the same as the theological language. Something more is present in the Christian speaking of Jesus than is given by historical awareness. After all, something more than historical accuracy is the condition for the religious life. Though theological language about Jesus ought not to be historically inaccurate, still His historical character and all the attendant detail is but a clue, a kind of sign, which both reveals and challenges the purposes and thoughts of men by forcing them to another kind of interpretation, one in which the quality of the observer is more important than the detail about the historical figure.

The fact that "God" is a concept which refers to historical things does not mean that everything said about Him is also historical. The language of faith is a very rich fare. It is full of propositions. This word is a logician's delight. It ought, again, to frighten no one, for it calls attention to a familiar feature of our use of language, namely, that we use words to assert something about something else. Concepts refer (meaning complexes refer), whereas propositions assert (meaning complexes assert). Most of theology consists in talking about God and talking about everything in the world in relation to God. The point, then, is simply that our religious concepts are historical, not ideal or imaginative, but our theological judgments are not historical judgments at all. Biblical studies might well permit us today to understand better the problems of authorship, of date, of text, of environment, but it is doubtful whether these are the necessary conditions for the enlightenment of conscience, the strenuousness of purpose, and all that is meant by the intensification of ardor. Certainly the latter, not the former, are the condition for the religious life and for theological judgment.

Simultaneously, then, Christians are oriented towards things historical, So, too, are the Jews and the Mohammedans. But there remains a cleft between what is said in an historical kind of speaking and what is said in a creedal and religious way. So, here we have another instance of a problem for a man with religious concern. Many of the historical advances must remain in the nature of the case religiously indifferent, even when their subject matter is ostensibly religious material. For it is one thing to scrutinize religious documents, even ones new to us as in the instance of the Dead Sea Scrolls, and another to scrutinize oneself with their help. The religious use of Scriptures is quite different than an historical examination of them.

III

The latest temptation to the unwary here is the Dead Sea Scrolls. They are, apparently, full of all kinds of things—everything from very old, complete texts, that of Isaiah, for example, to fragments which illumine and help patternize the rather sketchy knowledge of the transitional period and literature between Judaism and Christianity. I have no doubt that these discoveries are enormously important to historians. Among the new and interesting books of a learned sort being published today, there are few which rival those on archeology, and especially those on the Scrolls, for stimulating the jaded tastes of the reading public. Among the many comments on the Scrolls, that of Mr. Edmund Wilson is perhaps the best written and surely the most exciting, but not without its limitations. Mr. Wilson has done an excellent job in making legible the romance of the discovery, the refusal of scholars to believe that such material could be authentic, the ups and downs of the life of learning that were provoked by that epochal 1947 discovery. Certainly his book, *The Scrolls from the Dead Sea* (Oxford University Press, 1955) is a most delightful account, gracefully, even deftly, done.

But it is remarkable for other reasons, too. A chapter called "What Would Renan Have Said?" lets Mr. Wilson play over the issues I have already discussed. This chapter is about the debate between the scholars, some of whom leap to the view that vindication for certain extra-historical and religious and theological theses is now available through a new batch of historical data. Mr. Wilson, himself strongly inclined to views not too different from Ernest Renan's, tells you why certain of his inclinations are easily stimulated. But the very plenitude of the suggestive material ought to constrain the cognizers, and Mr. Wilson too.

It is a little humorous to see Mr. Wilson castigating the scholars, "so many of whom have taken Christian orders or been trained in the rabbinical tradition," who have been "inhibited in dealing with such questions as these by their various religious commitments." Mr. Wilson believes that these religious commitments have kept scholars from drawing a lot of the hypotheses, indeed anti-conventional, which he believes are suggested. The hero among the scholars, according to Wilson, is the one who dared to say that Christianity was "a neo-Essene quasi-formation." This is supposed to be the daring hypothesis. But surely the matter is much more difficult than Mr. Wilson admits. Certainly he is in no position to assert that the confirmation or disconfirmation of religious views is contingent upon or consequent to any kind of historical research. This flutter of enthusiasm among believers and unbelievers as a rumor floats over the barricades of learning is a little ridiculous. One time it was evolution, next round it was relativity, then Frazer's *Golden Bough,* then King Tut, then psychoanalysis, now the Scrolls. Some people would have the religious believers thinking that they ought to get out of the ship of faith while there is still time.

Surely this is the comic side of scholarship, the misuse of learning. It is matched by the view that now the matter is clinched, that now the real reasons for being a believer or an unbeliever have finally been discovered. When the Dead Sea Scrolls are used to flag a fainting religious enthusiasm, when it is suggested that God's mercy has now been better documented and His providence amply footnoted, one again certainly has to watch out.

Religion has a perfectly fabulous power to survive, as Wilfred Sheed, the Catholic publisher, has repeatedly said. It survives both its attackers and its defenders. But why this is so, is difficult to say. (Some people say it lives by grace.) The attackers and the defenders are invariably suggesting that historical research is now qualifying matters uniquely. All of this proposes, I believe, that a seriousness about the nature of historical research, a kind of objectivity and detachment, a willingness to limit one's talk to what the hypothesis is about and to be circumspect in expounding what it suggests, is still the better part of scholarship. And an intensive scrutiny of the roots of one's religiousness might be in order, too. Perhaps a little self-analysis by the faithful would show that relatively little personal religion is dependent upon historical research or that many convictions about history held within religion are not the kind historians hold as historians.

But more is in order than this, too. With all the talk about the Western religions being historical and the Eastern being non-historical, it still is not altogether clear what these assertions actually mean. It may be that Wilson's book and others like it, which raise questions about the origin of the Christian religion, the actual historical facts concerning Jesus, etc., will be doing a real intellectual and religious service. Perhaps it does not make as much difference as many people have believed whether Jesus was or was not an Essene. Perhaps this fact is as irrelevant to His being the Son of God as His being a carpenter's son or a Nazarene. But, just why this can be said, or cannot be said, raises important questions for reflective people. Wilson's book has the merit of touching our important loyalties and yet orienting our concerns simultaneously to some fundamental problems of scholarly research. Little more can be asked of an author than this, even if he does seem to have unnecessarily frightened the faithful with his diatribes.

If anyone enjoys learning at all he ought also to enjoy it for its own sake. The Dead Sea Scrolls are almost a test of sobriety, and great credit is due some of the sober students, like Professors Nelson Glueck and Millar Burrows. For the rest of us, as for them, it is not ours to panic one way or the other, but rather to enjoy the contemplation of one of the most thrilling discoveries of modern times. Perhaps after twenty-five years, or maybe more, the scrolls too will have been assimilated in circumspect ways into the body of knowledge. The part of wisdom open to all of us is to await that day.

CHAPTER FOUR

History, Providence and Faith:
Herbert Butterfield

One of the most versatile scholars in our day is Herbert Butterfield, professor of Modern History in the University of Cambridge. He is a practicing historian of outstanding merit, having written a short life of Napoleon, another book about him called *The Peace-Tactics of Napoleon, 1806-1808,* and still another long work entitled, *George III, Lord North and the People, 1779-1780.* These do not exhaust the genre, for several years ago he wrote a penetrating history of scientific thought, *The Origins of Modern Science, 1300-1800,* which discloses a breadth of interest and competence that is truly startling. However, these are less than half of his story. In addition to everything else, Mr. Butterfield is a kind of self-conscious student of his own craft. He does not only write history, but he writes very tellingly and voluminously about historiography and the science which historical writing aims to be.

In the latter capacity he has written *The Historical Novel, The Whig Interpretation of History, Christianity and History, History and Human Relations, Man on His Past,* and several smaller pieces too. With all of his other attributes, Mr. Butterfield exhibits an enthusiasm for the Christian faith, which occasions his speaking as a layman in churches of England, and probably accounts for his patient concern with the problems of faith as these affect the acting and writing of history. All of this finds expression in several detailed studies of the relations between history and being Christian, to which questions he returns in many different forms.

Professor Butterfield is what the learned world would call a philosopher of history. He is interested in the intellectual problems open to a person who thinks about the historical process. For one of the indubitable facts about people is that they are historical; they make history; they record it; they value the story about their past; and, without fail, they understand themselves to their own satisfaction only when they understand their own histories. One might say, therefore, that being historical is a diagnostic fact about people. Butterfield has an inordinate reflective interest in that fact.

There are, of course, kinds of philosophers of history, just as there are kinds of philosophers of science. Karl Heim (Chapter V), for example, is the kind of thinking man who apparently believes that it is essential to comprehend the largest and most inclusive patterns of nature in order to understand oneself therein. There are philosophers and theologians who say something analogous about the historical process. Arnold Toynbee is to the historical scene what we have here described Heim as being to the scientific. Toynbee is that kind of historian who looks for large patterns, the big aggregates, which seem to hold the numerous events of history together in ways that look meaningful. Toynbee has captured the imagination of many religious people of our day because he professes to find that historical sequences justify and even suggest faith in God. It is almost as if history is the court in which God is being tried and Toynbee is the judge. The verdict is seemingly that God is doing fairly well, that the evidence which historical events represent is on the side of vindicating the claims about His providential care of mankind.

There is something wistful and soothing about such magnificent intellectual efforts as Toynbee has essayed that is not to be gainsaid. But the criticisms of such efforts must also be heard —and the number of critics is legion. The school of thinkers called positivists are typically antithetical. They have raised pertinacious questions, particularly about the significance and relevance of such extrapolating efforts with the results of modern science. They have decried the validity of world-schemes constructed out of scientific materials and have, with others, insisted that people interested in reflecting about science ought not to synthesize the results of science but rather ought to analyze and clarify the concepts, the aims, and the bearing of whatever results are already obtained. Positivists have unjustifiably been thought to be atheists because of this delimited and programmatic view. Actually, however, what they have said on these questions applies only indirectly to religion. They are quick to point out that theologians who use science to prove God's existence are also introducing factors alien to the scientific results and that such an enterprise is not necessarily a worthy one. A philosopher of science who chooses to confine his reflection to the analysis of what scientists do and say is usually described as a critical and anti-speculative thinker.

One of the typical postures of men of learning is to refuse to put the pieces together into large totalities. Some persons are inclined to view the fragmentation of learning just as they do the divisions among nations—as if an ethical fault lies at the root of anarchy. But in the case of scholarship, it is fair to say that the difficulty lies in the sheer quantity and difficulty of the task. No available tools, logical or otherwise, seem quite adequate to synthesis.

Among historians there is a movement analogous to that among the natural scientists. A leader among such historians, or philosophers of history, is Professor Butterfield. As already noted, he is not irreligious; instead he makes a rather unequivocal profession of a lively Christian enthusiasm. Mr. Butterfield is, nonetheless, poles apart from Arnold Toynbee. Where the latter speculates and conjectures and even seems to be anxiously trying to prove that all things work together for those who love God, the former tells us the following: "Hold to Christ, and for the rest be totally uncommitted."[1] Butterfield never suggests that historical science proves anything important of an ethical or a religious sort. From one point of view, he does to history what the positivists have done to science, namely, declare its ethical and religious neutrality, but all this without quite being a positivist and always while avowing his belief in God and His Providence.

II

But there are several interesting sides to Butterfield's delineation of how history and Christian faith go together in an historian's mind. As an observer of large sweeps of time, Butterfield confesses to finding nothing in the knowledge of the past which completes a man's education. If one admits that everyone must search out an interpretation of life, that the hungry look of the man who is seeking an answer to the essential riddle of life is highly appropriate, still this historian is quick to say that no resolution of such a problem is available in historical knowledge. Unlike many historically addicted peo-

---

[1]*Christianity and History* (New York, 1950), p. 146.

ple, Butterfield does not agree that the lessons of life are clearer if the extent of awareness is increased.

This is as much as to say that grand schemes describing God's providential care in history are not as much a result of contemplating the past ways of men as they are interpretations which men have brought to history and which they superimpose upon it. This may seem a damaging charge to make against the fulsome views which historians and theologians have proclaimed. And Butterfield intends, in part, that the charge should be damaging. But there are some refinements in order too.

For one thing his charge cuts against all kinds of metaphysical schemes of history and not only the theological views. Anyone who dares to suggest that all the past adds up to the inevitable progress of men or that all of the past and all of the future, too, are only matters describable by economic and material laws is equally subject to the charge. Such historical abridgements are, according to Butterfield, never warranted by the historical methods open to the technical and exacting historian.

Besides the fault of a strictly intellectual sort, there is another, and slightly more evanescent, difficulty too. The despair of many people has perhaps even been increased by those historians who act as prophets and who misuse their competence as students of the past to increase the expectations of the unsuspecting multitudes respecting the future. Karl Marx is a notable example cited, but he is only one of the many who has dared to suggest that the realities open to the professionally trained observer of the past guarantee a more perfect community of men tomorrow. Surely Butterfield is right when he says that there are serious defects in the process of transmitting human experience and that historians have liberally shared these defects, even though many of them have admitted to the noblest of ethical and religious aims.

Correlative to this view of the matter is another, and one must admit, a subtly complementary point. For certainly it is true that every man wants and needs a total view of things. Every man is poorer without a general theory of the existence of which he is a part. Butterfield recognizes this fact and speaks of it very aptly. He argues that every interpretation of the human drama, of the "why" of the rise and fall of kings and kingdoms, is really an extension of the interpretation we give to our most private experiences. Thus it is that the large views are not demanded by the facts, not produced really by the evidence, but are an expression in a significant part of the sovereign decisions we must make about ourselves and what we choose to be. However, to admit this much seems almost denigrating for the historically inclined. On the other hand, Butterfield finds men altogether too willing to agnegate their personal responsibilities, to decry their personalities and the importance thereof, in order to blame whatever exists outside of themselves for their own views.

This means for the Jews and the Christians that God's ways among men are not open to the technical research at all. With other historians of the day, Butterfield argues that technical history can describe some events and occurences in ways which are valid, independent of creed, race or philosophy. But the claim that God rules the historical scene and that He entered it in the person of Jesus Christ—these are not matters of technical history and cannot be established by the evidence available. The upshot of this reflection for the historian is, consequently, a kind of scientific history, which Butterfield calls technical history, wherein the historians, limited by their kinds of apparatus and evidence, restrict their realm to the tangible mechanisms of historical change. This is the way Butterfield explains the rather obvious mundane and even pedestrian character of modern historical scholarship and narrative. From this kind of history, which can be, and often is, accurate and matter-of-fact, nothing of great moment can be expected, except the truth about a limited matter. But if people are seeking more, as most of them are when they ask whether they should be rebellious or conservative, Christian or infidel, warlike or peaceful, then it seems quite clear that history will not explain itself no matter how great the length of time studied.

It seems almost as if Butterfield is telling us why we cannot expect our salvation in the historiography of the race. If we do not know this before, we surely can read it in his pages. His diatribes are based upon a very exacting study of the making of the modern science of history, and it is with considerable learning and discerning logic that he concludes to the effect that no one will find God in the academic study of history who has not found Him in the actual experience of his own life. Put in another way, this says that the meaning of one's own life is no more apparent when one has promoted the study of history than it is in the interstices of one's own personality. And of the pretentious vanities, deceiving men into a contemplation of objectivities outside of themselves, history is accordingly one of the greatest and most particularly when it proposes the salvation of men.

III

Butterfield is yet another voice of our time who has called attention to the drama of personality. If he can be believed, God's arena is primarily the world of human relations, the inner life, or what R. G. Collingwood, another distinguished historian and philosopher, calls the "inside of events." Butterfield tells us in categorical fashion that the historian sees only the mechanisms by which events are brought about, the outside of the events, not the seat of personality in which the event is conceived and purposed. Therefore, no observer of natural or historical events can really document and trace God's role in the scheme of things. Without drawing on the theologians of our day, many of whom say this too, Butterfield tells us that God's availability is a matter of each person for himself, for each man associates with God in the small arena that is his own personality.

The augmentation of personality seems almost like a cult today. All kinds of people—poets, existentialists, theologians, and philosophers—seem to be saying that the inner life is all-important. But not everyone who speaks about it does so with authority. Butterfield gives his reader some well-defined ruminations on the subject. For example, from the point of view of the technical historian, he finds no discernible difference between the history of the Hebrews and that of other people. Before the reader rebels, however, he must pause a bit and discover what is meant. Butterfield is saying that God's guidance of the Hebrews is not evident, that all the claims to miraculous intervention, all supernatural guidance during the exodus from Egypt and the settlement of Canaan, all of these and more are not matters which the technical historian can conclude from his study of the available records. But one fact does stand out, and that is the historiography of the Hebrews. They tell their own history in religious terms and their faith shines through their written accounts. The Old Testament is an unique book because it shows what faith means to an historical people. Furthermore, such faith is an extremely rare thing.

Perhaps all of this is like a strange parable. Once men who were weak in faith and courage looked to men of great learning to help make their faith strong. How was this to be? Well, if it could be shown by scientists that God really made the world, or by philosophers that the world could have come about in no other way but by creation, if it could be shown by historians that God really led the Israelites, that He spoke to Moses as the Biblical account says, then surely men could have faith in Him and belief would thrive in the land. And so it was. Some scientists and some historians were thrilled by the prospect, and they scanned nature and history with objective discernment to find the ways of God. But their accounts were often inconclusive, and the disappointments among the aspirants to faith were numerous. So, new learning was encouraged, more scholarship and more objectivity, more money and more research, but still the riddle was not read and faith was still hanging. Men talked of making learning international, of paying the learners more, of giving prestige even before the accomplishment, but God stayed hidden and faith still seemed a terrible risk.

Time went by and there were mutterings by some of the faithful against learning, especially concerning the sciences, but there was still hope for the humanities and history. Some historians were obliging. They described the world as if it were all to God's credit, and especially did they find faith to be valuable in securing the survival of civilization. However, this was not the problem. For the issue never was the value of faith but its validity. Does God act in history so that He can be banked upon? Does He deserve the human credit? These were the real questions.

Finally the matter was treated rather decisively. Some men of learning said that learning about learning, about the sciences and history, gave the reflective man a clue to the limitations of knowledge itself. Perhaps, said these few, God is never objectively discernible; perhaps His ways are past finding out—though some of the more desperate ones insisted that "qua scientia," God did not exist at all! In any case, the upshot was the same. God cannot be known by the methods available to us. Therefore, it is a mistake to insist that the men of learning provide the grounds of faith, that they establish belief for the rest of the generation. This is one view that was correctly drawn. Among the men who said this were astronomers, physicists, biologists and the historians, who were the last.

But the view spread slowly and seemed almost impious. Almost it seemed to some as if the men of learning did not really care. But gradually another point came to be made, and it was that faith (Christian faith and also that of Jews) was really a test of the viability and strength of personality. Maybe something had been overlooked and maybe it was man himself. So another word got around—it was that the world was good in and by itself (there was an ancient story to the effect that God looked upon all that He had made and, behold, it was good!) and that persons seemed to have monopolized evil. Of course, there were aberrations within the view, but the total effect was a new emphasis upon the glory of being a man. And faith was no longer understood as response to something obvious and given, but was seen to be an act of God's grace. On the human side, faith arose in the face of objective difficulties and when all strength failed. Faith was also courage which came anew like the balm of Gilead. And these things were said by students of the Bible as well as others so that the thought was not alien to those who treasured the ancient books and the faith of the fathers.

Modern learning is something like this story. Professor Butterfield's role in it is a telling one because he speaks at once for both sides: on the side of history and science, he shows us

the limits of knowledge and why final causes and such purposes that might govern totalities are not intellectually feasible;
on the other side, he has discovered and stated the role of faith
with clarity and acumen. Few writers of our day have as much
to say as he does about the function and purposing of faith in
the personality. Faith is not elicited by the objective certainties but by the objective uncertainties. Butterfield shows us the
latter and says that they result because of both the very logic
and form of human intelligence and the nature of events. All
of this augments the role of personality and warrants Butterfield's claim that there is such a thing as a Christian interpretation of the entire human drama and that this interpretation
of existing is an aspect of religion itself.

All of this is part of an intellectual movement, profound
yet clear. No historical science can demonstrate the truth of
an interpretation which a Christian puts upon human events.
Put in another way, this means that there is an autonomy to the
person and his attitudes which enables him to make intimate
judgments about himself, his experience of time, and the course
of centuries as he has commanded it from historical scholarship.
To bring something to all of these as a Christian is to think and
to write as a theologian.

What begins as a study of the nature of human intelligence brings us in the end again to the role of faith and even
Christian faith. Perhaps the day is gone when Christianity can
be vindicated by learning. But gone, too, is the day when men
of learning can claim that faithlessness is a consequent of learning, that truth and belief are incompatible. The strategy of the
apologetics for faith is indirect—those apologetics reveal the
limits of knowledge and the place which faith can have. But
they by no means can produce it.

CHAPTER FIVE

Science and Faith: Karl Heim

In a work of huge compass called *Der evangelische Glaube und das Denken der Gegenwart* Karl Heim, of Tübingen, is again essaying the relation between the province of Christian faith and the provinces of human learning. In a spirit alien, perhaps, to much of contemporary European Protestant theology, and even to much of current Roman Catholic thought, the German theologian specifically discusses the results of contemporary learning and not the categories of knowledge. Thus his problem is not precisely that of relating reason to faith as this problem has lately been considered but, is instead, that of relating faith and its theological categories to the cognitive details, and generalizations from them, which concern the nature of man and the physical world. Karl Heim's efforts bespeak wide erudition and a skillful command of detail, both, of course, essential to becoming aware of the question as he conceives it. This should not lead the reader to expect the kind of analysis which is typical of post-Kantian philosophy and theology. What analysis there is, is expended upon the content and the theory within various fields of learning and not upon the forms of intelligibility nor upon the possible forms of religiosity.

Though each of Professor Heim's five volumes (and a sixth is forthcoming, all parts of the same work) has its own significance, I choose here to comment only upon Volumes IV and V, both of which clearly exhibit the argument of the entire work and, besides, so state the case as to overlap in appeal with the kind of issue with which much of Anglo-American literature is concerned. The two works are *Christian Faith and Natural Science* and *The Transformation of the Scientific World View*.[1] Readers of Heim's earlier writings are perhaps amply cognizant of his somewhat idio-syncratic approach. He seems to avoid addressing the communities of either the faithful or the learned in their own terms. But in these two volumes the problem he shares with both communities gives him egress immediately; and whatever the ultimate judgment about his solution, there can be little doubt about the pertinence of his inquiry. For, though both theological and philosophical currents are running against Heim, by denying the possibility of the dependence of ethical commitment or religious faith upon cognitive propositions, yet philosophers and theologians must continue to speak to the issue in order to make their negations relevant. And it is to this issue that Karl Heim speaks with great learning and at surprising length. In what follows I shall address myself to three considerations by which his work may be evaluated and described. These are, first, his problem; second, the presuppositions of the problem thus stated; and, third, a criticism or two.

---

[1]Both are published in English translations by the SCM Press, London, 1953. The first is Volume IV in the series and was published in German in 1949; the second, Volume V, was first published in 1951.

I

There is a certain sense in which Karl Heim is akin to Rudolf Bultmann. Both German theologians are troubled by the breakdown of the argument with which the Christian church addresses the world. They are concerned to diagnose the failure of communication and propose a remedy. For both men an argument must be dialectical and dialogical. An argument presupposes two points of view and two arguers. But the irony is that the church's dialogue is actually an instance of the church talking to itself, a monologue as it were. And there is no one to convince because no one is really listening. Bultmann finds that the Christian church has few listeners and few dialectical opponents because the *kerygma* is overlaid with certain components which, while seeming to be biblical, are yet mythological. Without the myth faith can be related to the believer more primitively and more nakedly than it can with the myth. Bultmann believes the negative task of stripping the myth from the Gospel message to be of positive theological and religious benefit; for it means that the accretion within which its relevance was once made evident for others is removed, and thus it once again leaves the faith-elements negotiable and accessible to contemporaries.[2] At this point Heim finds the difficulties to be more complex. Although a Lutheran-oriented believer who appears to be cognizant of Luther's vitality and pertinence, he does not find it sufficient to re-conjugate the Law-Gospel theme, nor does he believe that the *eros* and *agape* themes are sufficiently comprehensive to state an entire theology. Contrary to most of recent Protestant theology, he does not disparage (except with a considerable remainder) the theological and philosophical traditions of the seventeenth and eighteenth centuries.

[2]Ian Henderson, *Myth in the New Testament* (London, 1952). Cf. also *Kerygma und Mythos*, which contains Bultmann's original demythologizing essay and numerous critiques of it, and Paul Leo, "Kerygma and Mythos," in *The Lutheran Quarterly*, Nov. 1953.

What, then, is his analysis? He finds the current intellectual situation to be disheartening indeed. He believes that modern science and technology (even admitting war, and mass unemployment, and urbanization, and everything else that is "evil") have created attitudes and actions which make religious language and attitudes almost an irrelevancy. It is not that religion offends; it simply does not interest anyone, least of all the learned man. Heim's understanding of secularism allows him to say that the religious issue disappears when the contemporary picture of the physical universe is sketched by scientists and is understood and acted upon by others. Thus he says: "The church is like a ship on whose deck festivities are still kept up and glorious music is heard, while deep below the water-line a leak has sprung and masses of water are pouring in, so that the vessel is settling hourly lower, though the pumps are manned day and night."[3] This situation demands a very strenuous and systematic effort if the ship is to be saved. Instead of proposing a negative task for the theologian and biblical interpreter, Heim is intent upon the theologian again assuming a constructive task of synthesis.

Unlike others who believe theology to be confessional, Karl Heim wants to make theology polemical. He wants theology to plug the leak in the ship of faith! His intent in his entire work has been, and is, to strengthen the tactical arm of the church. He wishes to restore the vigor and enthusiasm and manliness of the theological enterprise. Apparently, therefore, he has no patience with those who, either in ignorance or with intelligence, do either of the following: (a) defend the totality of the church's teaching by isolating a part of it—a single doctrine, for example—and extending its persuasiveness to the totality, or (b) separate theology from learning by stressing

[3]*Christian Faith and Natural Science*, p. 24.

its independence. To do the first is to disregard the thoroughness of the scientific world outlook and to imagine that it is weak because another point of view, albeit the Christian, is strong in at least one area. Piecemeal attacks he finds vain, for secularism is rooted, both cognitively and attitudinally, in the "contemporary conception of the physical universe," and whether permission is granted by scientists or denied by theologians, contemporary men become secular in outlook. Even those intimate with theology and the activities of the church admit that this same secularism "traverses our own hearts."[4] In other words, the pervasiveness of the attack of secularism forbids the ordinary kind of critique and demands, instead, a wholesale and complete reconstruction.

In contradistinction to Bultmann, who believes that demythologizing the message is itself religiously important, Heim believes that worldliness and secularism have entered the thought structures of the learned and the ignorant, the believing and the unbelieving, and constitute the world insofar as we respond to it as an order. Worldliness is therefore not a negation, not an absence, not a void; it is something positive and with content, and it can be combatted only by something equally contentful and positive. To negate the secularist world view without providing another would be for Heim a travesty of intellectual and religious justice.

But the situation in Protestantism is even more refined than this, for since Schleiermacher, theology has abstracted some themes from the Scriptures and from history which seem to be always the same—for example, responsibility, salvation, sin, regeneration, etc.—and by developing these ". . . in every direction . . . has thought it could quite confidently leave all the

---

[4]*Ibid.*, p. 25. See also pp. 11-34 and the first few pages of *The Transformation of the Scientific World View.*

rest to the profane sciences."[5] Heim's point about all of this is that this tactic, which once appeared to be sound, learned, and even evangelical, failed because these same profane sciences have taken over the theological themes and left the churches without an audience.

This is, of course, a very serious charge, for it indicts not only the church and its theologians but, as we shall see, science too. For by giving up wrestling with cognitive principalities and powers, theologians have literally let the devil take over —and with the help, of all people, of the scientists! The German theologian is at pains to show that the lack of theological perspicuity and criticism, and the lack of an intellectual and religious dialectic by which opposition is made clear, caused men of learning who fed on the sciences to fill the vacuum with religious surrogates. Theological independence, besides its inimical effect upon the clergy and the pew, besides its failure to keep Christianity credible, was also an intellectual error. And insofar as theologians and scientists believed in the independence of the cognitive contents of theology from other disciplines, both shared the conviction that the whole was constituted by the part which they cognized. Though Heim does not say so, it would seem that this could be put in terms like the following; that an attempt to make oneself a whole man, a living synthesis, would fail if any part of knowledge (for example, either sciences about the world, or theology without the sciences and philosophy) would constitute the whole man.

The immanent and intrinsic requirements of the intelligence are therefore the other significant aspect of the problem occasioning Heim's writing. Because neither science (at least as it has been understood) nor theology has construed the part in the context of the whole, it is essential to effect a recon-

[5]*Christian Faith*, p. 26.

struction in both the theological order and the scientific, or perhaps it would be better to say in the meta-scientific order. Theology, from Schleiermacher to Barth, Lutheran or Calvinistic, is in need of a correction which the author finds possible only as one reassesses the scientific world view. This world view is scientific—that is, it grows out of the cognitive content of the physical sciences—and within its meanings is the nexus by which the content of Christian faith can be communicated to contemporary men. The changes necessary to make theology polemical again, and of tactical use, are not of the nature which would mean a modification of theological content, but they would be of an incremental and an additive sort; the changes necessary to restore intellectual and intrinsic merit to cognitive awareness are to be effected primarily by concessions on the part of scientists as to the merits and extra-scientific bearing of recent physical theory.

II

It would be a mistake to suppose that Karl Heim's many-volume work could be categorically delineated without a much more detailed analysis of ideas and terms than is offered in these few pages. Therefore, only a modest endeavor is here proposed, that of analyzing a very few of the attitudes which seem to be involved in the very mode of stating the problem.

First, and perhaps of most importance, is the flat assertion which, because it is asserted and not argued, functions as an attitude and not as a conclusion, namely, that "all responsible speech and action rest upon an overall picture of reality."[6] This is a very straightforward assertion, and like all obvious "truths" which, Heim says, "everybody today knows from experience," does not have to be repeated. But often such assertions are either empty banalities which tell you nothing at all, or they

6*Ibid.*, p. 37.

are simplifications of an otherwise complex matter which can
be understood to any degree of intellectual satisfaction only
when the complexity is described in many sentences rather
than one. For the moment, let us assume that we know what
an "overall picture of reality" is. Suppose that it is a kind of
sentence or group of sentences found in Genesis 1, or in the
assertion that "everything is made of atoms," or "all events are
determined." Professor Heim takes to be established (and believes that everyone knows the same by experience) what the
Sophists of the ancient world sought to establish against Plato
and Socrates and numerous other critics. This is the view that
the subjective life of speech and action depends upon a view,
comprehensive and full, of the way things really are. This has a
name in the history of reflection—Sophism. The point is that
it gives ethical, and in Heim's instance, religious significance
to knowledge of facts. Sophism in religion means that theology,
if it is knowledge of God, is conceived to be the cognitive
ground from which the Christian way of life is a deduction.
Any attempt to deduce a way of life from facts is sophistry,
whatever the facts might be. After Socrates' day the willingness
of teachers to accept money for teaching the facts while promising to produce virtue was used to give to sophistry another
connotation than the more epistemological one. Though there
is nothing obvious about Heim's sophistry—it is disguised here,
as it always must be—it seems to me that his theological work,
together with all theological works conceived in the same mode,
are instances of it.

If the contemplation of facts, of views, of even the world
itself can somehow produce a kind and quality of human existence, it would seem to be the responsibility of anyone who
insists on this to tell us "which" facts and "how." At this point
Karl Heim does not really carry the argument any further than

it was centuries ago. He provides the facts that he believes are important, but he says nothing about the "how," and here is where the difficulty lies. Of course, it is true that some facts startle the observer and others do not. But assent to the truth of a view about anything you please—God, the stars, astronomical distances, the life of Jesus, the occurrence of miracles, the piety of Mary—none of these by itself produces a view of life. Nor does any of them produce the same response in various beholders. What we mean by the truth about events is the endeavor to find that which we can state and agree upon, irrespective of the many qualities of response that are possible. Responses are various, not only to things and events, but also to the truths about things and events. Not all of these responses are a sole function of the things or the events. Some of them depend in large part upon the capacities of the observer. Aristotle discerned that the capacity to wonder was not evenly distributed among men, and other capacities for subjective response are equally differentiated.

The question which is raised by Karl Heim's work is whether or not truth-claims (or even the physical order thus described) translate into "responsible speech and action" directly. If so, are the quantity and the "overall-ness" so important? Or, is the translation indirect? Then, what are the elements essential to the indirect translation? Now, of course, if it is wonder that makes some people interested and amazed and attracted and attentive, then we enter an arena not commanded at all by true propositions or views. A picture of reality, whatever its proportions, is not then constitutive. Surely "wonder" is not an area to be commanded by any writer or his books. Oddly enough, Heim seems to admit this difficulty when he cites Fichte, who told his students to "stop looking at all that surrounds us and concentrate solely on ourselves. . . ."[7] Heim even avers that this is the only way to find God, who cannot be encountered by "objective contemplation of the great law-abiding complex of natural processes."[8] Rather than make the distinction sharp for the intellectual order, Heim chooses to address himself throughout his work to the notion that concerns about God and the self and concerns about physical research somehow overlap or intersect.[9] Hence, however sharp the distinction is drawn on the one hand, it is blurred and rendered useless for purposes of discriminating analysis by the supposition that knowledge of events somewhere and somehow makes a direct translation into a view of life and a quality of inwardness.

Related to this first presupposition is a second one, which is more difficult to state. Let us examine his argument and see if we can determine its intent. He looks at the physical sciences and finds three major changes produced by recent advances. The notion of an "absolute object" (a kind of thing or substance or existent which has qualities which we know and for which our words or thoughts or knowledge — the subjective response—are but an approximation) is no longer tenable, and for numerous subtle reasons which he is at pains to trace.[10] Belief in the fixed references of time and space for everything knowable is made impossible by the relativity theory, and the absolute determinism of natural events is negated by the a-causal concept used in modern physics.[11] Certainly Professor Heim is right in saying that the picture of a world of things, all related to one another causally and in a space and duration, which are their common measure, was (and perhaps still is)

[7]*Transformation*, p. 247.
[8]*Ibid.*, passim. Cf. *Christian Faith*, pp. 202 ff.
[9]*Transformation*, p. 112.
[10]*Ibid.*, pp. 27-64.
[11]*Ibid.*, pp. 65-168.

the view accompanying most scientific endeavor.[12] But granting this, Heim proceeds to erect another kind of extra-scientific world view which is compatible with recent science. In so doing he seems to disregard the salutary humility of many scientists who, on the ground of their awareness of the cognitive limits of empirical facts, refuse to generalize or hypostatize views or things which would mean a new metaphysics or a new world view. Even Newton was perhaps not empirical, despite his scientific proclivity, when he gave such enormous scope to space and time. And the criticisms of Newton's reflections were engendered by mathematicians on the one side, who found that the relationship between Euclidean geometry and existence was not itself mathematical, and physicists on the other, who found that the relationship was not observable. The destruction of the old world view was not so much the direct result of the growth of empiricism or empirical knowledge as it was an indirect consequence of the growth of knowledge and a correlative reflection upon the limits of knowledge. World views do not grow without a considerable extra-empirical factor being added.

Karl Heim writes as if the old science produced the old world view, and that the new science produces, in his own instance at least, a new world view. This is much too simple. Belief in an object, absolute if you will, is not a scientific matter. It is extra-scientific and becomes a part of science only when incorporated into the texture of scientific language, and then only by a kind of secular grace! The attempt to construct a metaphysical world view on the results of a science presupposes a kind of correspondence between levels of cognition that simply does not exist. It is possible to construe (even at this date)

---

[12]Whitehead's *Science and the Modern World* makes this point most clearly, and tellingly too. Cassirer has also explored this issue in a number of his writings.

the empirical results of science with various extra-scientific world views, including, I suspect, those which Heim says most scientists have rejected. Where the correspondence between empirical facts and over-views is so loose, and where, on the other hand, metaphysical views are so loose and so commodious that they will fit the facts of one generation and again the vastly incremented facts of another, another ground than the facts ought to be suspected as fundamental for all metaphysics. This does not, of course, mean that any given metaphysical view is false, but it does mean that verification for a metaphysical assertion does not lie in the facts in the same way as verification of a scientific hypothesis. Or one might say this in another way: because the facts are so ambiguous in respect to their metaphysical bearing (that is, they permit so many, or at least several, without requiring any single one), therefore one ought to suspect a non-intellective and non-factual ground for the metaphysical view. Though Professor Heim hints at this possibility, he never develops the suggestion; instead, in virtue of his argument, he creates in his reader the belief that a metaphysical view, or at least some of them, stand related to bodies of facts or whole sciences almost as hypotheses stand related to individual facts.

Again, lest I be unfair, it is incumbent upon me to point out that Heim does explore selfhood as Fichte had commanded and that he does come up with a kind of Christian world view. In fact, this is the burden of his volume, *Christian Faith and Natural Science.* He finds that the ego lives in a non-polar, non-objective space.[13] This contention, buttressed with countless details and reminiscent of much of existentialist philosophy, Heim finds to be incompatible with secularism but compatible with the transformed world view which recent scientific theory

---

[13]*Christian Faith*, pp. 159 ff. The argument is restated in somewhat different categories in *Transformation*, pp. 200-207 and 240-256.

permits and which Heim himself writes out. The crucifixion of the intelligence, which is thought to be an act of self-denial for Christian intellectuals, is a consequence of misunderstanding. It is only with the now out-moded scientific world view that the *sacrificium intellectus* must take place.[14] With the new and transformed view such a negation of intelligence need not occur. In fact, the continuity which is necessary to bridge the gap between the Christian and the secular is the same as that continuity which can restore integrity to the intelligence of the single knower.

The bridge is built from both sides. The Fichtean and existentialist emphasis upon inwardness and selfhood yields a religious content for Heim which is complemented by the metaphysics arising from the contemplation of scientific knowledge. The latter point must be remembered. It is not the nonsophisticated wonder of the innocent person at the immediacies of nature which yields the metaphysical harvest; rather is it the sophisticated man's understanding of the scientifically mediated facts which are the instrumentalities of the overall picture of reality. And the stress upon inwardness is also a stress upon introspective cognitive awareness or, more properly, upon awareness which seems in Heim's writings to be conceptual but is achieved introspectively. So, here again, the Christian and ethical source claimed by the author is another source of knowledge. Ethicality and Christianity do not have their locus within subjectivity, nor do they stand related to the individual in any kind of immediacy. Both, or together, they are cognitively encountered, and the "enigma of personal existence" becomes of maximal religious significance only when recast by the individual into cognitive forms. This is why it becomes so appropriate to insist that Heim finds the objectifi-

---

[14]*Ibid.*, p. 172.

cation of the intelligence religiously efficacious. Despite his overtures to other modes of stating the Christian faith, and to much of recent neo-Kantian philosophy, he still illustrates the presupposition that knowledge issues in metaphysics and that metaphysics constitutes the content of theological discourse.

III

There can be no doubt that Heim has been stung by the flexibility and toughness of secularism. His effort to understand it must necessarily be substantial and equally strenuous. The fact that he finds it so distressing is an indication of evangelical zeal that bespeaks a high degree of passion and enthusiasm. Certainly, too, he is right to look with anxiety upon the Christian's reluctance to understand the other man's best thoughts. Without his saying so, it is perhaps accurate to say that he finds that some Christians can evade the evangelical task with the best of theological reasons. And here he fights the theological dragons of the time as well as those who seek to devour the queen. But admitting all of this, is there not a reservation that must be made?

Suppose we reflect for a moment upon the fact that "space" and "time" were once considered to be meaningful because such words were believed to be names of actualities. This certainly was once a very common conviction. Suppose, too, that such words (because they were believed to refer to actualities) were useful. Suppose, for example, that they were used in persuasive contexts, in world views, and that "responsible speech and action" (as Karl Heim says) rested upon them. After a century or two, men find that actualities are not related to these words as their usage had implied. In fact, as Heim himself tells us, the use of these very words can be documented, and today we are no longer sure that there are corresponding actualities or that the words play any significant role. Is not this a good reason for practicing more austerity with respect to words—or shall we say metaphysics?—so that we do not attach our responsibilities wantonly? Or is it the other way? If responsibilities emanate from knowledge of actualities, and the actualities do not exist, then will we have no responsibilities? A good part of the history of science—and according to some historians, also a good part of historical writing—reflects the slow and very painful acquisition of an awareness that the multiplication of entities by metaphysical views is a gratuitous business. If this be so in intellectual endeavors, might it not be even more important to learn the dangers for the ethical and religious life? But all of this admitted, metaphysical words may still be important. They may reflect the user's attitudes and needs with respect to whatever actualities there are. Certainly it is not only the existence of an object which is important; the attitude one has toward the object is even more important. But an attitude toward an object where there is no object is somewhat ridiculous. The manufacture of objects by the use of words is equally ridiculous. The latter seems to have been the case with much of classical metaphysics.

Professor Heim is at great pains to give us meaningful examples of this from the history of science.[15] But at the same time he seems to carry on the project he condemns. For he seems to argue that words which have a function must also have an actual object. Thus he tells us that Christianity ". . . is intelligible only if an omnipresent space exists, which encompasses us all, no matter whether we be children or adults, average people or heroes, and by virtue of which there is a third possible way of existence, one that raises us infinitely far above the two possibilities, relativism and positivism, which lie open

---

[15]*Ibid.*, pp. 35-48.

to us within the polar space."[16] It is not at all clear how this non-objective, non-polar space is known to be actual. That the words have a use in Heim's writings cannot be denied. But the point is that he does not admit that he is expressing an attitude or re-aligning the known facts about nature and people to cohere more satisfactorily to his intention. Rather, he insists that he is constructing a scientific world view of nothing less than reality itself. The words about non-polar space are used as if they were descriptive. And, of course, this is why Heim believes the view to be religiously and ethically productive.

But nothing that Professor Heim says brings conviction to the reader whose doubt has been aroused on the point of whether or not there is an objective reference to metaphysical language. It is, furthermore, doubt that metaphysical language has objective reference that sustains secularism and indifference to the claims for God's existence. To fight another man on his terms is very sporting. But to fight within the circle of doubt created by reflection by using the very tools of reflection which initially produced the doubt, is to fight without a chance of winning. No, it would have been far better had the author's magnificent talents and even dialectical skills been spent upon a much simpler issue, namely, the reason for the rejection of what he calls the scientific world view of the past. He rightfully accepts that rejection, but instead of tracing the epistemological course of the argument, he speeds to the task (if one can speed in several volumes!) of building another metaphysical structure which is already vulnerable even without waiting for future scientific discoveries.

There is a further question which is relevant too. Has a Christian the right to persuade men of the truth of Christianity for wrong, albeit persuasive, reasons? Does a Christian who

[16]*Christian Faith*, p. 194. See also *Transformation*, "Introduction," and Chapter VI, Sect. 25.

wills to reflect have the right to bring others into the reflective arena and share only the certitudes and plausible conjectures to which reflection gives access? If the doubts are equally sustained by reflection and would mitigate the religious believing, are not the plausible conjectures wrong reasons for believing? And does not reflection presuppose doubt? Is not reflection itself thwarted without doubt? To admit a doubt is to admit that the metaphysics is also doubtful. And to say this is to make the movement of faith dependent not upon the certainty of the metaphysics, for this does not actually obtain, but upon factors within the personality which are not described within the objective picture of reality. If a man becomes a Christian or finds it easier to become a Christian because the scientific world view is true, he is then only scientifically superstitious. If a man becomes a Christian and makes the movement of faith because he finds no one world view necessary, then factors within his own subjectivity permit him to choose. The doubt which the objective world views permit, simultaneously permits the movement of faith without commanding it. Karl Heim's efforts, encompassing as they are, and learned and detailed as they also are, still do not credit personality with the capacity for Christian faith without the application of metaphysical certainties. With the state of metaphysics being what it is, might it not be a matter of wisdom to conjecture that it is the argument that is wanting rather than metaphysics which is wanting?

CHAPTER SIX

Society and Faith: Will Herberg

Barbara Ward, in a "Report to Europe on America," after another of her many trips through the U.S., said, "We did not need the evidence of polls or church attendance to confirm what we could so easily observe—the walls of new churches rising in town and countryside wherever we went."[1] What seems to be here but a casual impression is borne out amply by evidence. Church building, church attendance, church membership, the presence of religious books on the best-seller lists—these are certainly signs of a turn to religion on the part of American people today.

Simultaneously with this account comes another, namely, that of historians and moralists, which says in effect that the trend toward secularism is not, despite appearances, being reversed. While the enthusiasm for religion rises on the one side, the quality of that religion seems, to many observers, to be thinner than ever. Therefore, many leaders of religious organizations and students of the trends in American historical development are inclined to say that the contemporary religious upsurge, if such there is, is a fake.

---

[1]Cited in Will Herberg, *Protestant, Catholic, Jew* (New York, 1955), p. 13.

The presence of these two views does not necessarily mean that another logical contradiction or paradox is being foisted upon the public. For, it is altogether probable that there is an upsurge in religious activity, and, also, that current religion is only a disguised form of secular interest. Some authors are inclined to the view that sociologists can adequately explain contemporary popular religion by recourse to laws of society, including what is otherwise thought to be the Holy Spirit's or God's impetus in their purview. Others are inclined to think that modern religion, as distinguished from some earlier forms, is only a reaction to the insecurities of our political and economic life and, if these were removed, so would be the religion.

One thing is clear enough. There is not much unanimity abroad on the character of the current American revival of religious interest. Though piety is all for saying that it is because of the need for God, the sense of guilt, devout and holy purposes, there are disturbing rejoinders that keep getting their wide hearing. All of this is in keeping with Mr. William Miller, who, in a couple of biting articles in one of the journals of opinion, suggested that a lot of negative thinking about Norman Vincent Peale's positive thinking was in order, and further, that the new "piety along the Potomac" was politically and socially more useful than it was personally needful.[2]

Maybe this is just another way of exploiting a certain vulnerability of religion. Persons of any kind of faith claim to be affirming, standing for and with something, that seeks to mold the behavior and affections of men. As David Hume said long ago, "It is infinitely easier to defend the negative." Perhaps the negative is simply getting its inning once again. But a second look is disconcerting. Many of the critics of American religiousness are themselves religious persons. Not all of them are

[2]*Reporter*, Aug. 17, 1954.

the intellectuals, the theologians, who find it easy to pick flaws in the more mundane endeavors of rabbis, priests, and pastors. Instead it must be said that many of the critics are men of religious persuasion, cleric and lay, theologians and otherwise, who find that the current *éclat,* the trend, is religiously trivial while simultaneously being socially very impressive. These are the people who are insisting, from within religious communities, that religious life cannot be judged by the criteria of numbers, finances, and social utility.

Few people writing in this mood have said it so well as Will Herberg. Mr. Herberg was formerly an educational officer for a labor union. He is not a professor by training. He is now a lecturer and writer by vocation and an ardent Jew by persuasion. He has written an earlier book, *Judaism and Modern Man,*[3] which proved him to be theologically and philosophically adept and, besides that, an expert about and a practitioner of a major religion. Numerous articles in a wide variety of journals, religious, sociological, political, have come from his pen during the last ten years. The book, *Protestant, Catholic, and Jew: an Essay in American Religious Sociology,* published in 1955, will undoubtedly add to the measure of his stature. It is in this book, three hundred and twenty pages of text and bibliography, that Mr. Herberg scrutinizes American religion in earnest.

What he has to say is not entirely pleasant. For purposes of this essay, I want to emphasize primarily his evaluation of the return to religion. Readers of his book will find Mr. Herberg summarizing many detailed studies of American Protestant groups, of the history of American Catholicism, of the evangelical movements, of Judaism and its indigenous forms, of the Reform movement, of Conservatism, of Orthodoxy and

---

[3]The subtitle is "An Interpretation of Jewish Religion." (New York, 1951).

its problems, etc. This book represents solid scholarship and discriminating analysis, the fruits of some of the best historical study done on American immigration and social life. But the point of the book is not made in the descriptive account of how American religions got to be where and what they are. The point is rather made in Mr. Herberg's judgment that in getting to where Americans are religiously, they have lost a lot of their religion. Mr. Herberg believes that we ought not to be so extravagant in our praise of the current scene. Mr. Herberg's thoughts about the developments are most taxing, and it is here that he seems to make a major contribution.

I

First, there is the fact that Protestants, Catholics, and Jews, in differing proportions, to be sure, are all caught in the same cultural push. All three religious groups, with admitted differences between and within them, have not resisted this cultural and social push but instead are building, expanding, and also, in subtle ways, accommodating to each other within it. Jewish worship reflects Protestant practice; the Roman Catholic Church has made and continues to make concessions to the American ethos. Not all of this, or any of it, is intrinsically bad. But Herberg's point is that all three groups are now characterizable as *American*. There is something distinctively American, rather than Irish or Scandinavian, ethnic or dogmatic, about religion in this land. The theological differences, he seems to be saying, are doing less to separate Protestants, Catholics, and Jews, both from one another and from the nonreligious, than the peculiar *American-ness* of prosperous religion is drawing them together. Amid the asseverations of the theologians and the restoration of distinctiveness to theological and religious belief, Mr. Herberg finds it a little strange that the protocol of the churches tends to obliterate the significance of the *religious* views of life. His point is that this is not a denominational, not a local phenomenon. The major religious emphases in America threaten to become progressively more *American,* at the expense of whatever else they profess to be.

Such a phenomenon would be unimportant were it not for two other relevant considerations. One is the fact that ethnic loyalties still characterize the forms of some religious groups. Some of them are still separated from one another, as are the Lutherans, by habits and liturgies which were once as decisive as the differences between one country and another. Herberg's story makes clear that sociological developments have often been more rapid than our overt willingness to admit the changes. Immense differences in fact then are being socially obliterated, while assertions of these differences continue to alienate peoples, one from another.

But the other and more important matter is the fact that Christians and Jews have always claimed to be moved by supernatural powers. If one claims to be conditioned by the unconditioned One, Who is righteousness and truth and the Holy God of our fathers, then it must be the case that a sign of that religiousness ought on occasion to be visible. However, Herberg and others remind us that modern religion of the American sort does not lead to Jewish and Christian distinctiveness, to distinctive postures or stances. Instead, the religious groups tend to become so conditioned by America and all of its energies that they are no longer separated at all. Whether this is an improvement in any serious religious sense is a moot point. No longer alienated by ethnic and linguistic differences, the religious groups now are synthesized into the American melting pot, but with a high price being paid.

With the process of assimilation to American life has come

the destruction of religious distinctiveness. When one remembers that the theologies of modern religion, the new Biblical emphasis, the re-assessment of orthodoxies and the repudiation of the optimistic liberalisms have all credited the theme of the Bible, that believers should come out from among them and be separate, then again we can see how theology really does not guide the churches to the extent that is often asserted.

II

Second, admitting that responsiveness to the sociological situation is not altogether wrong, Mr. Herberg yet charges that American religion, Catholic, Jewish, and Protestant, is creating something new, a *tertium quid,* an American religion. Quoting President Eisenhower, who said in early 1955, "Recognition of the Supreme Being is the first, the most basic expression of Americanism; without God there can be no American form of government, nor an American way of life," Mr. Herberg says that here our President was speaking for the mass of American people.[4] Yet the mass of Americans are still getting their religion in Catholic, Protestant, and Jewish forms. But what are they getting from their religion? Surely the most crass of observers might admit that there are mysteries of religious communion and incommunicable values of private prayer. But with it all, Herberg says, a *new belief* is being fostered, a new set of credenda is coming into existence. From Presidents and the religious leaders on down to the masses, who are for religion whatever the kind, there is a conviction, a growing one too, that Catholics, Protestants, and Jews share a common spiritual foundation of basic ideals and wants, the chief of these being religion itself. This is a *common* American religion, common, as it were, to Catholic, Protestant, and Jew, and found not so much in their respective teaching, if at all, but

---

[4]*Protestant, Catholic and Jew,* pp. 274-275.

rather as a slowly accumulating lore, an accompaniment to the practice of religion. Mr. Herberg thinks this is really, as he calls it, "an underlying culture-religion," neither Jewish nor Christian, a kind of sentimentalizing and poetizing of "the religious aspect of the American way of life."

This is not theologically defined religion nor is it oriented to the Biblical heritage of the Judeo-Christian tradition. Perhaps it is akin to what Catholics are accustomed to calling natural religion or what Cicero in ancient times named civic religion. The anomaly today is that it thrives under conventional supernatural labels. Perhaps the words of Eisenhower describe it best when he said: "Our government makes no sense, unless it is founded in a deeply felt religious faith—and I don't care what it is."[5] Whatever else can be said for it, Herberg's thesis gives one sober pause. For it may be that unwittingly we are allowing our religious institutions to become the organs for our national unity, and once again we may be depriving ourselves of the pearl of great price. A tribal religion may be the bond of the people, but it surely would never be the faith of Abraham and Isaac, Jesus and Paul, nor perhaps some of us, if we took cognizance.

III

This new business, American democratic religion, tends to become also the means whereby Americans sanctify their own culture and society. Seen in this perspective, American religion is not something altogether new. But it may be novel, as Herberg suggests, citing numerous authorities, that religions as diverse as America's should combine so effectively in producing a *civic* religion like the modern one. Surely Roman history tells us of an emperor's religion which made political revolt almost impossible, and the histories of other nations are testi-

[5]Quoted from *New York Times* (Dec. 23, 1952) in Herberg, *op cit.*, p. 97.

mony to analogous phenomena. But, in America, cultural pluralism and wide religious differences, not indifference and unanimity, seem to produce a new piety, the American way of being religious, of which the three faiths previously noted are but alternative and variant forms. Mr. Herberg thinks this is a loss to religion, whatever the gains it may mean to Americanism. Instead of being salt in the body and leaven in the lump, instead of providing the judgment of chauvinism and the critique of pride and bluff, we seem to be creating a kind of religiousness which validates society and culture, which justifies it in advance by identifying it with the divine purpose.

As strongly as many proponents might deny all of this, Herberg supports his view by many facts which gives plausibility to his thesis. He cites the poll-takers, who have measured the average man's convictions, to indicate that most men are not getting the distinctiveness their theology teaches in the modern religious bustle. Even if one avers that religion is good for everybody and denies vociferously that religion is Americanism, it seems clear from this volume that Americanism is more distinctive of many Catholics, Protestants, and Jews than the Judeo-Christian tradition and its strictures upon worldliness, naturalism, and self-righteousness would allow. Furthermore, what is coming through to the laity in modern religion seems much more attenuated than what is being offered at the religious source. With modern theologians rediscovering the insights of the past, with the new understandings of faithfulness and guilt, there is a terrible loss between the source of the teachings and their absorption. It is this loss that makes this such an interesting study. For it is American sociology, the account of other causes and purposes in the American people, and not theology, that gives Herberg the clues.

Another noteworthy characteristic, and perhaps related to

those already mentioned, is the fact that there are few admitted atheists and agnostics today. Herberg laments the fact principally because he finds the introversion of belief reprehensible. There are few, if any, Darrows and Ingersolls who dare to be publicly against religion. Surely not everyone who is against it deserves a hearing, any more than everyone who is for it. Herberg's point is rather that religion has become so much a part of the ethos of American life that anti-religion is almost inconceivable. But if one is for so little in being for religion, how could anyone conceivably be against it? If being against religion is like being against America, who cares to be rebellious when the American way of life still seems so attractive?

With a word of caution, perhaps it is in order for everyone to think about Herberg's question. Is our religiousness without a religion, without content? His contention is apparently that most of us use religion only as a guarantor of our sociability as Americans, and not for very much more. This is a striking charge to make but, like most charges generated by religious insight and enthusiasm, it means relatively little until we apply it to ourselves. When we do this we cannot examine our neighbor, for he is his own business. It is ours to know ourselves and repent of our misuse of faith. We are reminded by this book that we are not required to have faith in faith or really to believe in religion. As Christians we ought to say with the Jews, "Our trust is in the Lord from whence cometh our help."

IV

Granting for the moment the truth of Herberg's claim, we ought also to exercise ourselves in another way. The very nature and use of theological views is part of our question. Herberg's analysis is a description of our common religious life, and he finds that theology is not taken very seriously. But what are the conditions for taking theology seriously?

It certainly is true that Catholic theology aims to relate believers to God via a particular institution, the Roman Catholic Church. Jewish teaching has another goal, and Protestantism still another. No one reading all three could say that they are all doing the same thing. If it is true that these teachings are no longer determinative and that other energies in our common social life are determinative, then a re-evaluation of the pedagogical function of theology and other forms of religious teaching are in order. But right here the differences between theology and other kinds of teaching begin to obtrude. The purposes of teaching theology have to fit the subject matter which is the religious life. These purposes have to be remembered always, otherwise we begin to mark failures where there were none.

An example from another area of discourse might help us. In teaching geography, for example, the truth about land masses, seas, and climate can be stated in language which is clear, specific and adequate. That language can be learned, for the language does not deceive. With a little care and diligence in formulating the concepts, the language soon bears its burden well enough. If another person hears the words, he can learn directly what is being said. The sign that he knows the subject matter is whether or not he can state the truth for himself. One fulfills the aim of the learning by knowing how to use the language. Even the examination systems that are used to test command of a field of learning are instructive, for they show us clearly that there are devices for assimilating, using, testing the objective truths that have been proffered.

Theology is another matter altogether. A theological statement, even a piece of the creed, is supposed to be an expression of a religious consciousness and life. To be able to speak in theological manner means being able to refer everything to

God. It supposes that one has the enthusiasm of faith, the encompassing zeal of the faith, by which everything becomes new and different. Therefore, a religious expression, whether Jewish, Catholic, or Protestant in origin, is not about something and that alone. Such expressions are both about the world and, correlatively, of the person. They are both objective in their reference and scope, and subjective in their genesis. Even the creeds begin with the somber note, "I believe." The sciences are articulated impersonally and detachedly. There the rubric is simply, "The facts are . . ." The hope is to make language a kind of mirror of the world, a kind of corresponding truth about whatever object one chooses. Truths of scholarship and science are not an expression of their author's subjectivity, unless the discipline is undeveloped or the particular topic is new or bizarre.

Therefore, it is a moot question not only *what* people believe but also *how* they believe. For theological believing is largely a matter of *how,* not *what.* This might be said in another way. To believe a sentence about something, even a religious matter, means that one assents to its claim. If a person says, "Yes, I believe that," we have little reason to ask whether or not he means what he says. For *meaning* the act of belief, or simply believing, when the object of the belief is a proposition *about,* is not very complex. It is pertinent, of course, to ask whether a person understands; and it is an obvious enough maxim that one should understand before he believes. But, respecting the language of faith, the creeds, the Bible, and the confessional documents of one's church, the issue becomes quite different. Here, saying "yes" is not enough. Even saying that you believe is not enough, for what marks the difference between language about faith and the language of faith is the fact that the latter requires a deep enthusiasm and a consuming passion. Religious language is only appropriately used when the speaker has a corresponding spontaneity and inwardness to match the expression. Theological language, thus, requires the *how* on the part of the speaker; without the *how*, without a properly qualified mode of believing, the *what* of that same language is lost.

When students of American mores tell us that a new religion has come into being, it is an apt time to ask just what that means. It may be that a new theology, or at least, a new language of the human spirit has flourished among us. America, after all, does have its glories; and it is small wonder that hymns and declarations have arisen to sound the thankfulness for opportunity, for a new life, and for advantages dwarfing those of nations left behind. This, too, is a language of enthusiasm, of thanks, of praise, even of hope. Therefore, it looks like a theological kind of speech, and sometimes it gets decked out in histrionic rubrics, almost churchly. Can one be certain that this has replaced the theological teachings? It does not appear to be a clear and precise matter to determine.

It would seem that what is in order still is that peculiar kind of nurture that must go with the revival of theology. All of us must learn about the religious life and its requirements, for only in the travail of living a life of prayer and devotion can we encompass the *how* of believing. We suffer not so much the lack of theology as we do the ruled life by which to use it. Perhaps we are reaping the consequences of indiscriminate teaching of religion, almost too much of it, and now most of us must learn how to put it to its edifying purposes. This is, perhaps, why otherwise distinguished people can mangle it so easily, why it can be modified so grossly, why it can be forgotten so quickly. Instead of accusing everyone in general, perchance we ought to look carefully at these teachings before blurting them thoughtlessly to the rest of mankind. Instead of mass exposure to a host of sayings which can scarcely but remain idle, maybe we ought to look at one or two of them and see what they require.

In lieu of further castigation of the present situation, peradventure we ought to renew our task, especially if we are teachers of morals and religion. On the other side, too, there is a task awaiting us. For patriotism also lacks shape and proper expression. It is simply not true that in order to be patriotic and deeply moved by loyalty and gratitude to one's country that one must be quasi-religious or so speak as to confuse one's religious fidelity and its expressions thereby. With all of the interest in faithfulness to one's country created in these past few years, we seem to have forgotten that the *what* is not adequately discussed until we see the *how* clearly. A little attention paid to these matters is not an aside at all; rather, it brings one to the heart of the matter.

Mr. Herberg's pages are a reminder of how shallow our faiths really are. But those same pages tell us that patriotism, despite its fervent champions and ardent defenders, is shallow too. For if we can confuse faith in God with loyalty to America, this indicts both our national and ecclesiastical leadership; and if we can applaud expressions which confuse God and country, we still have much to learn.

CHAPTER SEVEN

Faith and Belief: Martin Buber

Few living authors on religious themes have received such wide adulation within their lifetime as has Martin Buber. His early and very slim book called *I and Thou* has given impetus to countless essays, a new direction to numerous arguments about the Judeo-Christian conception of faith, and even a fresh conception of the faith-reason issue so long discussed in traditional philosophy and theology. Martin Buber, long a distinguished spokesman for Jewish religion, a kind of philosopher speaking out of the harassed community of Old Testament believers within Nazi Germany, and more lately a professor of philosophy at the rejuvenated University in Jerusalem, has made Judaism an immediately relevant religion, a lively option, not an antedated or superceded faith, not simply the old faith to be construed versus the new. Buber's authorship covers a variety of fields and topics—Jewish literature and tradition, Hasidic mysticism and lore, theological problems, reflections on the Old Testament and the New, and always a kind of philosophy, a kind of reflective and critical inquiry into persistent root questions.

Martin Buber is a gentle and non-argumentative sort of man. He lacks that characteristic bumptiousness and polemical spirit so widely praised and even sought among intellectuals, particularly philosophers. Every one of his books displays an irenic and kindly spirit, one unruffled by opposition and intent upon illumination of his opponents and not their conversion. Though Buber does not lack technical abilities, still he is not adept at logic or at easy symbolization of his ideas. He writes with a kind of leisure, a naturalness of style, that indicates a strong dose of common sense and perhaps a learned detachment from the ways of his fellow intellectuals. It is almost as if he has used his extraordinary abilities—for they are awesome in proportion—in order to think his way back into communion with his fellowmen and not least, the fellowship of Jews. A kind of profound and ethically conceived democracy governs Buber's attitudes and also his pen. He never seems to use his abilities to widen the breach between himself and the non-intelligentsia; instead he is intent upon using his pen, even as a Jew must use his life, to heal the breach between men and nations.

No one can profess competence in the technicalities of current religion, in contemporary theology and philosophy of religion, without knowing about Martin Buber. Now a venerable old man of letters, he seems something of a sage, a man of wisdom and of faith. He is neither naive nor sophisticated in the invidious sense of either word. He writes with a charming simplicity, almost as if he were not a professor at all, about matters for which others always create special vocabularies. Accordingly he has had a wide reading audience, of Christians, Jews, and, I suspect, literate people who are not sure whether they are religious at all. Buber has been a journalist, a civic leader, a kind of apostle of a wisdom-like faith, and a professor,

Thirty-five books, countless lectureships, the injustices of the Nazi vilification, a world-figure—all of these weave the fabric of the life of Martin Buber.

II

A simple distinction is made by Buber in his book, *I and Thou*. This distinction accords intimately with that described by the book, *Two Types of Faith*. Therefore the two books will be considered together.[1] The issue in the earlier book, *I and Thou*, is whether the relation between God and man can be described as a relation between a knower (man) and an object. As an approximation, this relation may be described as the familiar subject-object distinction. Does man, the subject, have awareness or cognition of God, the object? This is not an easy question to phrase significantly or to answer pertinently. Like most religious believers, Buber knows that language traps most people into saying, without reflection, that God is an object, and that men do have subjective and psychological awareness of that object, at least in so far as they believe. At this point, Buber makes a suggestion. He conjectures that the relation between God and man is not as the language suggests. Even if talked about in language that suggests cognition and a knowledge relation, the relation is of a different sort. At this point language is deceptive.

Out of a rich history of concern with the Old Testament and Jewish religious movements, Buber is bold enough to conjecture that the philosophers and theologians have been misled. He finds that similarity in modes of speech have led people to conclude that the relation between God and man is analogous to the relation between any object and man, the knower.

---

[1] *Ich und Du* was published in an English translation by R. G. Smith (Edinburgh: T. and T. Clark, 1937). *Two Types of Faith*, translated by N. P. Goldhawk, was published first in English, subsequently in the original German (London: Routledge, Kegan and Paul Ltd., 1951).

Unfortunately, the misleading power of this analogy does not end there. For the problem of faith itself is then wrongly phrased too. Almost numberless people, having been convinced that God was an object, there to be known, have conceived their own religious lack almost as they would a state of ignorance. To be without knowledge of any object is to be in a state of ignorance respecting that object; to be without knowledge of God is to be in a state where one cannot believe and, hence, is to be faithless; therefore, to be without knowledge of God is the root of the religious difficulties of any man.

All of this is to Buber a huge mistake. The fact that it seems to be almost built into religious talk, Catholic, Protestant, and Jewish, does not dissuade Buber at all. What is wrong is the elemental characterization of the relation between God and man. Here Buber says simply that it is a relation between an "I" and a "Thou," and hence the title of his book. The object, if such there is, is not an "it," not an object in the way epistemologists talk about thought having objects, but is rather a "Thou." This somewhat honorific English pronoun conveys, I suspect, fairly adequately the meaning Buber gives to the expression *du* in the German language. Buber's thesis is not that God might not have the status usually given to objects. God may exist; in fact, for Buber He is. The thesis is rather that God and man, religiously conceived, are related as are two *persons,* friends, shall we say. Two people who are related as friends, as companions, are not related as "I" and "it," as an "I" and an object. In fact, the more that relation is said to be *personal,* one in which love, regard, forgiveness, respect, and mutuality exists, the more inappropriate it becomes to consider the other as an object and oneself as subject.

More particularly, it might be pointed out that there are people about whom we have a kind of objective interest. We exercise detachment and restraint in relation to them and never allow ourselves to become attached or devoted. In fact, we fight, under some circumstances, the tendency to let their interests become our interests because then we lose our perspective and disinterestedness. Such a relation to other persons, or it may be to things too, would be an "I" and "it" relation, in which the other is an object, and the self is correspondingly objective. Surely Buber's view of epistemology allows this kind of illustration. By contrast, then, is the interested relation in others. When we love someone, we let our interests grow and even correspond to the person. In this relation, we do not care to know about an object as much as we care to do and to be what the person is. Knowledge is not the aim, but communion, fellowship, and affection are. Buber's view of the matter of religion is that we have let ourselves be overwhelmed by the repute of knowledge into thinking that God and man stand in an "I-it" relation. Theology itself has been falsified, and piety has been maligned. Buber's gentle argument is to the effect that religion must be conceived, not in analogy to knowing about things, but in difference from it.

Buber contends, and correctly, that religious language is misconstrued if it is assumed, a) to reflect primarily the view that God is an object and the knower a subject, and, b) that religious language is cognitive in virtue of the same rules whereby other language is cognitive, and, c) that even if God were an object and men could know that object, that that awareness describes adequately either the mode of religious knowing or the characteristic of being religious.

III

This seems a highly appropriate and long overdue highlighting of difficult matters. Religious people have certainly wanted to claim knowledge about God and especially when the rules for knowing seemed lax enough to allow God to be an object. But critics of religion, particularly the philosophic scientists, trying to disclose the minimum essentials permitting cognition, have leaped to the view that if there were no cognition under stringent conditions, then there was no legitimate religion at all. Buber steers a middle and difficult course. There is religion, he notes, for there still are Jews and Christians. But the question is whether the talk of religion and God has been correctly described. Are people religious because they have knowledge of the object first? Then, by acting discreetly and appropriately towards the object, do they become truly religious? Buber says no. People stand in "I-it" relations when their concern is the description of the object; they stand in "I-Thou" relations when their concern is that of the friend, the appreciative lover, the sensitive enjoyer, the thankful, interested, and regardful "I." Religion is made out of this kind of relation to the world. It presupposes the non-descriptive, non-cognitive subject, the *ich,* the "I," who is not seeking a description of any object.

But now to the second book, *Two Types of Faith,* a companion piece. It is a kind of extension of the earlier book. It is a clarification of the meanings of the word *glaube,* "belief," or "to believe." In the English language the most usable word is "faith." But the point, translated how you will, is that believing (or faith) is not all of one kind. When someone says, "Churchill is an old man," and another says, "I believe" or "I don't believe that," this is not the same kind of faith as that operating in the person who says "I believe in God Almighty," or "I believe in that man," or "I believe in Buddhism."

According to Mr. Buber's earlier analysis in the book, *I and Thou,* there is a kind of faith (or belief) appropriate to the "I-it" relation. When you describe an object, whatever it might be, you believe or disbelieve, as the case might be, the *sentence,* or body of language about the object. A person believes a sentence is true, for example. Mr. Buber does not say with certainty that there might be no such true language about God—he leaves some matters unsettled. His point is that religious believing or disbelieving is oversimplified if it is thought to be assenting or dissenting to language about God. His point is that religious believing is, and now I revert to the text of *Two Types of Faith,* like trusting someone, believing in someone, even if you are unable to offer sufficient reasons for the trust. Being faithful is more like this kind of relation than people have admitted heretofore.

This is how Buber accounts for the dissatisfaction that religious people have always felt with their interlocutors. Religious believers want to say that they believe, but they want to say that this is a different kind of belief. Martin Buber's comment is to the effect that there is indeed a difference in quality. There are two kinds of faith, two qualities or types of faith. He does not say that in the instance of cognition you believe a little and in religion a whole lot, or that in one instance you believe about objects which do not matter and in the other about objects which do matter. The difference is not in the importance of the objects, nor in the degree of commitment; the difference is a type-difference. All of the categories are dissimilar.

Even though Martin Buber's thought appears to have influenced Christian theologians almost more than it has Jewish theologians—or at least the "splash" has been larger among the former than among the latter—still it would not be true to Buber to suggest that this is a way of construing Christian faith, and that primarily. To the contrary, Buber's argument is that the type of faith noted in trusting someone has "its classic example in the early period of Israel, the people of faith—a community of faith which took its birth as a nation, a nation which took its birth as a community of faith." The second kind of faith, mistakenly assumed to be religious, the business of believing the truth of sentences, grew up "in the early period of Christianity . . . as a new formation, from the death of a great son of Israel and the subsequent belief in His resurrection . . ."[2] As Professor Buber sees the matter, faith for the Jew is more like a "persisting in" the community, almost like faithfulness in a marital relation; for example, staying true to the "I-Thou" relation posited in one's existence. Faith for the Christian becomes not "persistence in," but a "conversion to," and, in order to propose an object to which one must be converted, that object must be correctly described. Thus it is that Christianity, by making fidelity to another object, Jesus, the *sine qua non* of religious faith, seems required also to assert that "so and so is true." Acknowledging this, or at least some truth, seems the minimal religious act. Again this was aided by certain Greek modes of thought which the Christians embraced. Mr. Buber is intent in his book to show us that certain Jewish thinkers were also tempted by the canons of Greek rationality to surrender their fidelity in the "I-Thou" relation, their faithfulness to the community, not necessarily for the Christ, but for the new type of faith, the kind which would make the noetic factor most important.

But with all the complexities admitted even in advance, Buber's way of talking about religious matters has high value. It has changed the focus of the problem, enlivened all kinds of otherwise dead issues. Buber is the first to admit that Jews and Christians do not "in general" represent either extreme today. Each of the two has extended roots into other camps also. The

---

[2]Both quotations are from *Two Types of Faith*, pp. 9-10.

fact that the preface of this book expresses at length Buber's indebtedness to Christian theologians, including Albert Schweitzer, Rudolf Bultmann, and Rudolf Otto, among others, indicates a level of discourse from which all who can read might well profit. Few Christians have mastered the details of the New Testament as has Martin Buber. Few writers seem to have stated so well the problem of faith and believing for Jews and Christians together as has Martin Buber.

But the question posed by all of this is a very barbed one. Is it the case that Christians have lost their *religiousness* by what they have gained *intellectually?* Buber argues not for the Jews; his argument is rather that the fidelity-relation discovered in ancient Israel is the only kind of relation, and the kind of description too, that does justice to either and both, Jewish and Christian living. It is this point that stings a little and deserves a great deal of attention.

IV

Professor Buber's comments, aphoristic rather than argumentative and closely reasoned, are really a kind of meta-theology. Just as metaphysics was initially a literature coming after physics, so his pages come after theology. His proposals are not theological as much as they are about how one should consider theology and religious language. Buber correctly notes that the language of faith, not least that of the Old Testament prophets, is in a different idiom from that of textbooks and the classroom. He wants to make the idiom clear, so that irrelevant and meretricious language about God, the ceaseless speculation and countless cognitions of divinity, will be seen for what they are. Though Buber is not without ability to speak in a deeply religious idiom himself, yet his reflections about two kinds of faith and two kinds of relations are in the language about faith, not the language of faith.

There is an oddness about this position. Buber does not say that there is no "I-it" talk which is religious in content. His own literature, at least in part, belies such a strong claim. Rather is it the case that there is no knowledge about God in that kind of form. The very structure and shape of the Old Testament language and much of the New Testament, too, is in the "I-Thou" pattern. From all of this, one can surmise that much, if not all of the "I-it" language, subject-object speech, which is at all religious, is critical rather than constitutive or constructive. Buber's thought here is a second-degree kind, another level, not itself immediately religious in content.

It is almost as if Buber has looked long and hard at the perennial questions raised by philosophers and skeptics. Does God exist? Is there knowledge of God? Is God a person? Is God good? After patient inquiry and long exposure to the Scriptures (Buber has translated the Old Testament into contemporary idiomatic German), Buber has concluded that the very questions are wrong. It is not that the old answers are in error and that new ones are needed; instead, we need to read the Scriptures to discover what the issues of life actually are. It turns out that we are not in the advantageous position of being knowing subjects respecting God. Our questions are not altogether respectable, they do not belong to the religious context. But there is still a slim value in being objective about these matters; for, in thinking about the Old Testament and the faith of the prophets, one discovers that discipline and order make a difference. One discovers what is permissible and what is not. One learns the rules of the religious life instead of the answers to ponderous questions.

But saying this much leaves some dissatisfactions. How does it happen that religious men talk about the world and everything therein? How does it happen that they speak with such assurance about the earth being the Lord's? Certainly the user of such speech is proposing the truth about God and the world. Buber's remarks are here disquieting. Does he mean that there is no knowledge of God whatsoever? Because he is opposed to dogmatic theology, is he opposed to the confidence that a religious man has when he speaks about God and the world?

It is one thing to note the discontinuity between an objective interest, an intellectual curiosity, and a religious enthusiasm and faith. Certainly, there is a pronounced logical difference, a disproportionateness, between the language of each. This much Buber helps us to see by example and precept. But Buber tends to push this difference to a point where it ought not to be pushed. The fact is that religious consciousness is different than the cognitive consciousness. All that is meant by saying this is that curiosity dominates in one instance, religious passion in the other. But the religious consciousness also tries to relate everything to God. Men, even if religious, can not stop thinking and talking. Deeply religious men, mightily moved by passionate love for God and their neighbors, continue to speak. Their language has to be heard. It is one thing to note that religious men are related to God in a different way than they are to most objects. God, for example, does not satisfy curiosity and fill out the theoretical designs of various students. So it is correct to show that the Old Testament is not a series of answers, albeit garbled and poetic, to erstwhile cognitive questions. But it is another matter altogether to insist that, therefore, the Old Testament authors did not know something in virtue of their faith.

There is a charm and a clarity about Buber's lesson that ought not to be gainsaid. It is a mistake to treat religious literature as if it were only disguised and imperfect knowledge claims. It is absurd to construe it as if it were on the same scale as scientific talk. And, if the Apostle Paul is guilty, then he is guilty. Surely it would be the better part of wisdom to keep ordinary believing clearly demarcated from religious faithfulness. This does not excuse the oversight however. For the Apostle Paul, along with religious men of the ages, dares the conjecture that the whole world is related to God and His purposes. He says that he knows some of these things. This is the source of dogmas and theology. It may well have been a mistake for later dogmaticians to suppose that because there is an analogy between religious language about God and the world and ordinary convictions about the world, that therefore, the analogy extended even to the modes of interest, the kinds of consciousness, and the acts of faith or belief.

The difficulty is to keep the dogmas really religious in function and use. Buber wants to discard them altogether and to substitute another style of reflection and way of speaking. The more pertinent way is to keep the dogmas, for their source is the religious life, but to warn the hearers about their use. The language about God cannot be appropriated directly, no matter how refined and sophisticated the language might be. Every individual in turn must make the language about God, the dogmas, the language of his own faith, a personal expression. This is the abiding requirement levelled against the teachers of religious faith, lest they forget what being religious means, and against the pupils, lest they forget that the real teacher in human life is God, not a professor.

CHAPTER EIGHT

Culture and Faith: Romano Guardini

In the *Dublin Review* for 1949 a reporter, commenting upon his experiences in Germany, said that "the undisputed focus of intellectual activity in Tübingen is the lecture hall of Romano Guardini." Italian born in 1885, Romano Guardini early went to Germany and has spent his maturity there as a professor-priest. He has been a lecturer and teacher at the universities in Bonn, Breslau, Berlin, and since 1945, at Tubingen, and on occasion in Munich. One of the most impressive of men intellectually, he has been often cited too for a quality and kind of compassion. This latter facet of his personality was noted especially by numerous contemporaries who saw Guardini in the awful days of Nazi suppression and war. He is apparently both polemic and polite, critical and charitable.

All in all this man seems to be something of an enigma to the rest of us. For one thing, he has, even at an advanced age, almost boundless energy. He lectures continuously and almost everywhere. He is a founder and sustainer of the German Catholic Youth Movement. He is the author of fifty-plus books. He is an undisputed leader in German cultural and social life, an intimate friend of Konrad Adenauer and one of the authors and sponsors of the idea that Germany ought to pay reparations to the Jews it had persecuted. He sums much of this up himself by saying that he is one of those "uncomfortable Catholics"—a lover of St. Augustine, Pascal, and St. Francis, and a despiser of the irrational, of modern myths, of Wagner, and of German nationalism.

Guardini has deployed his energies very successfully in his teaching too. Many of the rising intellectual and cultural leaders of contemporary Germany admit a debt to him. His books will surely extend his authority as a person even further. He has written a volume of essays on Pascal, Kierkegaard, and Dostoievski, a book on *The Death of Socrates,* numerous technical philosophical essays, several lengthy meditations on the life of Jesus, and in addition, a host of pieces, long and short, on the culture of the twentieth century. But the book described here is not nearly so pretentious as the rest. It grew, as much of Guardini's work has, from "the concrete and historical situation." Originally this volume, called in English translation, *The Faith and Modern Man,* was printed as twelve separate essays. They were written during World War II in Germany, when hostility to religion was pronounced. Guardini felt that young people of Germany were being systematically deluded. With the thought-control system being what it was, new books were not feasible. Guardini therefore published these essays as booklets, designed to be enclosed in letters to soldiers. The subject matter of these essays could properly be termed in English, as Guardini himself says, "pondering the Christian faith." The essays are inquiries, attempts to assess and to evaluate; they are really *essays,* or kinds of trials and tests. The pondering was done, in part, in a series of lectures in a Berlin church during the dark days of the second World War, when lecturer and hearers were threatened from within by the secret police, from without by the air raids.

No one could hope to summarize so deftly written a book as this one, nor can anyone claim that it adds to the total stock of learning, that non-advocating learning, which is so easy to commend to any and all. The reasons for noting this book here are several, but the principal reason among them is the fact that the book discloses very clearly how a religious person thinks, and thinks well. He would be the first to point out that not everybody thinks or, if he does, thinks clearly. In an earlier day psychologists of religion talked about a religious consciousness. Today men would settle by saying that there is a religious language. In any case, Father Guardini is no amateur. He is an excellent example of a religious man thinking. His is a religious consciousness and he talks freely in religious fashion.

Many people who speak about "thinking" misunderstand what thinking is and means. Sometimes the textbooks on logic and "how to think" do an injustice to the process of reflection. They make it appear that it is always systematic, invariably according to rules, always directed towards goals, usually a matter of deduction or induction. But the fact of the matter is that little reflection is actually like that. Most of the time our minds work in a random manner, from one point to another, with extreme casualness typifying most of our activity. It is only afterwards that we begin to apply the rules and search out all the connecting links, and this in order to justify our conclusions and validate our results. And it is a mistake to equate the elaborate process of justification and logical argumentation with thinking itself. The justifying acts of thought are specialized instances of thinking but by no means the only instances.

People do in fact think and many of them think a great deal. Often those persons who say that you cannot think and be religious are confused into believing that because one cannot justify everything one believes in religion by the rules that govern some believing, therefore there is no reflection possible at all for religious people. Father Guardini is a good reminder that this is not the case. He is not the best illustration of the technical thinker, the man who construes every contention in logical forms, but he is a remarkable thinker in the sense noted above, a man who can convert his daily life and its experiences into ideas and language. And in this sense, religion actually causes a kind of reflection that no other attitude or view of life can cause. There is a distinctiveness to religious reflection that is very marked. One should not, therefore, be surprised that there is a distinctiveness also to the language of deeply religious people.

II

Father Guardini is, we have said, a candid example of a thinking man. Besides, he knows how to use religious language. He does not use it in place of scientific language, nor instead of poetry or poetry instead of it. Reading even this brief volume occasions the view that religious language (and the convictions so many people believe it states) has its own intrinsic qualities and province.

As an instance of his casual-appearing thought, we find Guardini saying that Italian Catholicism is too unthinking, that the film is culturally significant, that Protestantism smacks too often of a nationalistic religion. For such a panoply of convictions stated with ardour and even brilliance, Romano Guardini has been often praised, and as often perhaps maligned. Detesting sham and fraud, he has lashed out at superficial Catholicism, unreflective "believing," and the ever-present temptation to let religion be a Sunday matter. All of this has made him the target of criticism, of course. His enthusiasms (and perhaps extravagances) are highlighted in the following quotation:

> Living faith means dynamic life. Everything, every principle and every commonplace must be questioned. We must start from scratch and think every problem through from its very premises to its last implications. We must never rest with what we have achieved, we must never rely lazily on a "given" truth . . . A truly Catholic life is not the easiest and most satisfying, but the hardest, the least comfortable, and the most demanding. The more seriously we take [it] the more tasks and obligations await us.[1]

Father Guardini's book is an excellent illustration, albeit in an unintentional way, of the way in which religious language "means." In a day when a little learning is spread over so large a number of persons, it is also the case that a little skepticism is also spread over large numbers. Many persons, exposed to religion via parents, via the groups into which they are cast by chance, tend to forget that religion too represents a longtime community, a concentration of interests, a matrix of behavior patterns, a constellation of convictions, a pattern of discipline and devotion. Though comparisons may be invidious, it is almost as if many persons today tend to judge religion by standards incommensurate with its character and aim. For example, a certain amount of exposure to talk and to practice is necessary before one can know what science is about. And though it is said that science verifies and confirms in virtue of sense experience (surely this is what the *cognosciendi* like to say), still it is only the fool who would reject a knowledge-claim because he could not find the immediate

[1] *Faith and Modern Man*

sense experience. The intellectual life has its history, its community, its commitment pattern, and one does not judge the speech of learning until one knows something of it. Romano Guardini's essays remind the reader that neither the assimilation nor the rejection of religion is an easy matter. The use of religious language requires participation in the religious life and this involves exposure to the community of believers. Mind you, Father Guardini is not using this as a dodge. He is not escaping the difficulties. He is something like Pascal, who wondered how it was that any man could be so negative and so certain after reading one book and hearing one lecture. Guardini is telling his reader that no one is doing an honor to religion, and not least the Catholic faith, by rejecting or accepting it so cheaply.

In this respect Guardini does a service to Christianity and all of its forms on the descriptive side. His is no tawdry apologetics, no obviously plausible polemics. He is asking only that attention be paid to the detail before an affirmative or negative judgment is made. The disclosure of the detail is no mean accomplishment. Furthermore, in a day of cheap grace and easy talk about faith and God, it is very salutory to find a religious man telling us how expensive, how demanding it all is. It is almost as if he had discovered the good reasons anew for saying that one's body ought to be a living sacrifice.

III

But there is another side. Just as nations in time of trouble seem to settle for the most cursory kinds of loyalty, so the churches of the world are continually inclined to settle for a superficial kind of attention and faith. This surely is a vulnerable side of organized and institutional religion, and this, too, is Guardini's claim. Faith becomes a catch-all, an easy way out, as patriotism sometimes is. Guardini points to the conflict of religion and science as a case in point. In the past some scientific hypotheses created for religious believers a certain kind of crisis. Quick to defend the faith, religious leadership pointed out that science "mistook certain facts and evolved erroneous theories."[2] This may have been true, but Guardini does not let the point rest here. Scientific endeavor might correct its own errors anyway, he notes, and only slight praise is due the religious authorities for antedating scientific criticism. Exultation is here premature. Guardini says the difficulties between science and religion persist also "because Christian thought regarded as belonging to faith things that did not. Christian thought had failed to allow science sufficient scope, and held as component parts of faith views derived from scientific themes of an earlier age . . . Unenlightened lazy faith must take its share of blame as well."[3]

This is surely the vulnerable side of religious life. Guardini is very acute on this matter. Whenever a view is challenged, he says, an argument must ensue, that is, providing what one is saying is advanced as a thesis to be believed for reasons and/or in virtue of evidence. And Guardini is certain indeed that intellectual aggressiveness has no surrogates. Religion can only survive among reflective people if reflection itself goes on. Religion cannot stop reflection. If it does, as has sometimes happened, then the web of religious talk is torn.

But there is more to religion than talk, than argument, than conclusions drawn from premises. Again there is another vulnerability of religion but this is of another kind. Faith disappears when the moral practice which religion requires has disappeared. Guardini says that religion, and again he specifies the Catholic religion, requires an inner transformation. "If this inner transformation does not occur at all, or if it occurs in-

---

[2]Ibid.
[3]Ibid.

sufficiently, there arises a contradiction between conduct and faith which causes faith to collapse."[4]

Now these are very difficult matters. But the substance of them seems to be that religious conviction, belief in the conventional sense, is only psychologically possible when there is a kind of moral obedience (and this is specified) in the would-be believer, and further, that what one believes is also credible only when the language stating the beliefs somehow reflects or mirrors or affirms behavior; in this instance, religious behavior.

Therefore, though unbelief is, in part, often a matter of moral vagrancy (this has been said often enough), there is more to the matter than a superficial consideration might bring to light. The very language of religion lacks its meaning when religious morality in the believer is gone or is describable by means of other and non-religious categories. Religious belief and language cannot be separated from the morality and inner life of the believer. To separate them is to do violence to what religion aims to be.

Here it is clear that Guardini finds the culture of any time and place to be intimately bound up with the belief capacities of persons. Often the view that religion is implausible can best be understood as the protest of an acculturated man against that which looks anti-cultural and anti-intellectual and even, in some cases, positively immoral. Guardini argues that religion is vital only if it produces its own culture. Obedience, devotion, extravagant morality, fitting judgments and thoughts —these are ingredient to the cultivation of the Christian. Without them, in believers and skeptics alike, faith in God and Christ deserves to wither away. If faith has no substance, if the Christian religion adds nothing to the content of action and

---

[4] *Ibid.*

thought, then it is a superstition and can be said to be hostile to existing. The difficulties all of this proposes for the sophisticated are innumerable. Guardini is convinced that most of the attacks and defenses constructed for religion reflect simple ignorance. His arguments propose a higher degree of seriousness, more detailed knowledge and emphatic powers in those who discuss the faith.

Suffice it to say that Guardini is more suggestive than conclusive. One thing is very clear, nonetheless. Faith is extraordinarily complex. By saying that faith is not merely this or that, Guardini has succeeded in convincing his readers that it is both this and that and much more besides. To remit the beliefs while retaining the morality, as did Matthew Arnold and so many others who wanted to be up-to-date, appears to be a bit of fatuousness on the part of the learned. To admit the beliefs and to talk of the ways of God while living the pedestrian ways of men, is the faithlessness of the faithful. Faith is, even for modern men, a new kind of integrity. Because it is integrity it is also rare. Faith is no more out of date than is integrity. Guardini's diatribe against the world as well as the church is to the effect that this integrity is no longer properly discerned to be what it is. Because men are replete with a diversity of powers and drives, there is a continuing case for the ordering of men. Guardini is bold enough to assert that the new life in Christ is a kind of wholeness and unity which is not of men but of God.

Guardini's analysis credits another long look at the definitions of faith to which we have fallen heir. For a long while the Christian Church has lived on borrowed capital in this respect. With the vast stream of knowledge flowing in upon us, we, as Christians and reflective people, have been content with too little. Though the past is not to be denounced nor its heroes forgotten, still it is the better part of wisdom to revere the past and its men for our sakes and not theirs. A Catholic, wisely versed in tradition and the power of history, boldly tells us that faith is more than our learning has told us to be the truth. If this is so, then it behooves us to keep our learning adequate to the faith. We can only do this when we are willing to rethink our faith, not to deny its power, but to see it in relation to all that is. Guardini reminds us of the Bible's insistence, that faith issues in works, in a new creaturehood, in the abnegation of worldliness. The transformation in Christ involves us in the passion to bring the entire world into God's redemptive process. Whether Protestant or Catholic, this is faith which moves men to be no longer conformed to the world.

CHAPTER NINE

Catholicism and Protestant Faith: Karl Adam

About three hundred years ago, one of the brightest men of modern times began a correspondence with some French intellectuals. He was Leipzig-born, but in the 1670's he was librarian and historian for the House of Brunswick in Hanover, Germany. His interests were broad enough—he thought that perfecting his own reason and that of others, promoting human welfare, and loving God were all of a single piece. Having extraordinary talents and most exacting taste, he gave himself to the most abstract and detached of studies (those which we would term, perhaps, studies on the foundations of mathematics and logic) with precision and care, and also with passion. His stakes were as high as they could conceivably be—he thought that morality could be enhanced by intellectual exactitude and that the love of man for man would be increased by the satisfaction of the desire for truth. This man was Gottfried Wilhelm Leibnitz, surely a luminary among even the great ones of his century. But he noted several obstacles to his dream. Even though he believed God to be the creator of both the things in the world and our ideas of the things, and even though he thought God to be also the resolving and integrative factor for his proposed "universal calculus," still the worshippers of this God were disharmonious. They were Catholic and Protestant. Therefore, he sketched for Bossuet and Arnauld, his French correspondents, a proposal for the reunion of Catholic and Protestant churches.

There have been numerous integrative schemes proposed since, as almost anyone knows. And these plans have reflected good will and nonsense, hopes and fears, often ignorance, ill-will, and misunderstandings of the cause of division. In Stuttgart, Germany, during the summer of 1947, a conference of persons interested in the *Una Sancta* movement met to hear a professor of theology at Tübingen University deliver some lectures. The professor was Karl Adam, the renowned author of *The Spirit of Catholicism, The Son of God,* and *Christ Our Brother.* With a happy facility for conciliatory words, a candor about faults and abuses, and a sympathy for what he called "a bridge being built between Catholics and Lutherans," an *unio caritatis* (union in love) even if not an *unio fidei* (union in faith), with all of this he delivered himself on the possibility of the reunion of Christendom. These lectures were subsequently published by the New York and London publishing firm, Sheed and Ward, under the title, *One and Holy.*[1]

This is a day for bigger and better churches. In America, at least, where the ethnic and somewhat parochial motives for keeping churches separated are rather quickly disappearing, it is common to read about the "National Council of Churches" or a "National Association of Evangelicals." The somewhat pious hope that there will be a single Lutheran church body, rather than so many synods and groups, is kept alive by countless conferences, and Methodists, Congregationalists, and Episcopalians also keep up the integration "esprit."

---

[1]Translated by Cecily Hastings, 1951.

Even on a world scale, there are large movements, ecumenical in character. All Christians seem to be of single mind on the question of ecumenicity. Catholics and Protestants alike have ample motivation for making the church world-wide, universal, and general. Ecumenicity means nothing less than this, and every federation of churches, like the Lutheran World Federation, the Roman Catholic Church, the World Council of Churches, aim to represent the whole Christian world. The difficulty in all movements engineered by people is manifest in church politics, too. The motivation leading to the unity of the Christians are sometimes complex. A power-drive, ethnic and national pride, peculiar proclivities towards sovereignty of ideas and practices—all of these and more combine in church life, too. Sometimes, there seem to be leaders ready to sacrifice almost anything for the unity of men. The odd kind of hankering after unanimity that possesses some people always has to be balanced against the rights of individuals and groups to be richly differentiated. Especially is this true for Christians where solidarity of mankind is probably a lesser good than the renewing and repentance of a single sinner. All of this is said to indicate, however, that not everyone opposing ecumenical movements is necessarily bigoted any more than everyone sponsoring them is necessarily pure of heart and blessed with singleness of aim.

II

The interest of Karl Adam, like that of most Catholics, is firmly directed towards theological re-unification, though not exclusively. He writes, as he speaks, for a European situation, where the religious cleft is not obviously ethnic, not quite or exclusively social, not quite a difference to be erased by time, by changing customs, by more rapid acculturation. One can not deny the role of these factors. Still he writes not about them but about a difference, a break, which is theologically "justified"—and I use the word "justified" with a little discrimination.

Perhaps it is fair to say that many differences that are being ameliorated by unification and larger agglomeration in America were not created by theological argument in the first place, nor are they sustained by argument now. Whatever makes for plurality and differences, at least among Jewish groups and among Protestants, is often something other than theological points of view. It may be, too, that the differences between Jews and Christians, between Catholics and Protestants, are already being attenuated or brought to lesser effect by the peculiar social and political forces in America. This is what some authors, notably Will Herberg, are already arguing. But Professor Adam, writing within Germany, sees a difference between Catholics and Protestants (particularly Lutherans) which only discourse containing inference, i.e., argument, and argument about God and men, can state. With Catholicism thriving in America, it behooves American Protestants of good will never to underestimate that historic theological discourse. It was, and is still, argumentative because it contains inference; and, it helps to create the major cleft, that between Catholics and non-Catholics, by which Christendom was rent in twain.

As a reaction against over-intellectualized views of man, which construed human behavior as a conversion of ideas into practice, we have suffered in the last several decades an almost wholesale disparagement of ideas altogether. Many historians and sociologists, especially those describing big social movements like the Reformation, the French Revolution, and the origin of constitutional government, have so stressed the economic interests, the inclinations towards satisfaction of needs of every conceivable non-intellectual sort, that ideas have come to seem almost a triviality. In religious circles it has been fashionable to stress everything but theological convictions as motivational. Certainly Luther's desire to marry, the German princes' economic interests, the avariciousness of Papal legates have to be considered when writing about the Reformation; but to discuss these without the theological beliefs, or to assume that the theological beliefs were only thin disguises— and for all of the participants—by which motivations were made acceptable, this is absurd. Karl Adam is a sane historian. He admits the complexity of motivations, while treating most seriously the role of intellectual argument.

Karl Adam has little to offer those Protestants who believe Catholics are bigoted, or to those Catholics, in turn, who think all non-Catholics must be misinformed. Suffice it to say that Karl Adam himself is an informed man. He is an established Catholic theologian, an able writer and expositor of the claims of Catholicism. On the other hand, he knows that there were "roots" of the Reformation, that certain policies and practices fed a kind of inference and made probable an argument against the authority of the Roman Catholic Church. Furthermore, this argument, by itself, seemed compelling to many who heard the discourse. It is perhaps a tribute to Karl Adam and to the health of European Catholic opinion that such a recitation of factual conditions can be given in an irenic book like this one. Adam does not deny the abuses the Protestant Reformers talked about. From this fact, it is quite clear that the differences within Christendom do not, therefore, depend upon one side noting the abuses and the other denying their existence. Surely it is both pleasant and significant to have that superficiality penetrated. The Reformation was not simply a consequence of the virtuous being offended by malpractices, nor, on the other hand, was it the work of persons who exaggerated and lied about the behavior of others. There was an actual occasion for the breach. Professor Adam is very resolute on this matter. The facts are facts, and he refuses to countenance the views that parties to the conflict in Christendom have expressed, namely, that the occurrences were not as reputed and that simple honesty about the state of affairs would heal the breach.

His first chapter is, therefore, a disclosure of the "roots" of the Reformation. And there are roots. I quote Professor Adam:

> It was night indeed in a great part of Christendom. Such is the conclusion of our survey of the end of the fifteenth century: amongst the common people, a fearful decline of true piety into materialism and morbid hysteria; amongst the clergy, both lower and higher, widespread worldliness and neglect of duty; and amongst the very Shepherds of the Church, demonic ambition and sacrilegious perversion of holy things.[2]

But now, what about Luther and the Reformation? It is German Protestantism, that stemming from Luther, which concerns Adam most. Perhaps both Catholics and Protestants would be surprised to learn that this "ground-plan and centre of the Christian message (which) forms the core of both our Christian confessions" is the same.[3] After all the thunder was over, after Luther's break with the Roman Catholic Church, what was left? The "ground-plan and center" was identical. Even the Augsburg Confession, the first major document stating the beliefs of Lutherans in authoritative form, was more melioristic, as Professor Adam reads it, than most have been led to believe. In fact, its polemical and anti-Catholic sections, its recitation of abuses to be corrected, are "only things which in the Catholic view do not belong to the unalterable 'regula

[2]*One and Holy*, p. 25.
[3]*Ibid.*, pp. 54-55.

fidei,' the sphere of faith, but to the 'regula disciplina,' sphere of ecclesiastical discipline, which the Church could, if she saw fit, alter."[4] This is not to say that there were not, and are not, differences, and important ones too. But the point to remember is that Luther began with abuses and that the earliest *theological* arguments (the discourse containing the inference) were not contrary to the *regula fidei*.

Professor Adam is a little surprising among theologians, at least to the non-theological reader. Obviously a man of culture, of discriminating exactitude, he is more intent upon the irenic and friendly interpretation, if it can be found, than upon the polemic and opposing one. Perhaps like almost any person of great charity and intelligence, he discounts the prejudicial views right and left. In fact, reading this little book takes a great amount of fun out of the reiteration of the Protestant's case against the Roman Catholic Church. For here is a man who states that case more clearly than most Protestants do, and besides uses Catholic authorities to do it. Nowhere is he so adept at attenuating crude Protestant enthusiasm as in his treatment of the notion of "salvation by faith alone." After a page or two of tussle with that one, dear to most Protestants and a veritable theological war-cry, one is ready to credit Adam's assertion: "In fact, the phrase 'salvation by faith alone' has never been alien to Catholic theology."[5] There are more claims which are relevant too, especially those which begin with the disarming expression: "It was, in fact, always Catholic teaching that . . ." which claims are the means of showing that the radical departure averred by Protestants is not radical in quite the way that most of them say. Luther's thought, it is here

[4]*Ibid.*, p. 56.
[5]*Ibid.*, p. 59.

asserted, contains "wide tracts of thought" which were simply Catholic.[6]

Karl Adam is apparently one with European Protestants in going back to Luther himself. This is a most singular feature of contemporary Protestant religious thought, viz., the recovery by very exacting scholarship of the insights of the early Reformers. Karl Adam suggests that the later theologians of the sixteenth and seventeenth centuries were responsible for the wrong, or at least most of the wrong, theological inferences. Luther used abuses as his measuring stick and sought to heal and renew the ancient church, not to dissolve and destroy her. While it is customary for Protestants to belabor the sixteenth and seventeenth century theologians because of the manufacture of very elaborate metaphysical theologies and a consequent decline in the supposed Protestant spirit, here we find an author belaboring them for other reasons. Protestant orthodoxies were bodies of discourse, arguments, if you please, containing the inference which was strongly and purposely anti-Catholic. Not to be outdone, modern Catholic theology consequently determined itself by an equally earnest anti-Protestant polemic. All of which means that instead of abuses being corrected, today an opposition is "felt and understood more strongly by the theologians than it formerly was by Luther himself." Is there any wonder that a rapprochement between Catholicism and Protestantism will only be possible "if it takes Luther as its starting point?"[7]

Maybe this is all romanticism? Is the source purer than the main stream? Sometimes one cannot help but wonder at these waves of enthusiasm moving over even the scholars. The "back-to-Luther" and "back-to-Calvin" movements are surely major ingredients in the restoration of Protestant theology to the rank

[6]Note especially, pp. 54-76.
[7]*Ibid.*, p. 68.

of a discipline. But it seems a little strange that what the Protestants urge as the means of keeping the protest vivacious, Karl Adam urges as the means of beginning the reunion of Christendom. If Professor Adam is right, both can be done at once. He, too, is for the protest against abuses; his contention is that argument, the theological discourse containing the inference, is wrong. The first he finds in the Reformers, or at least in Luther; the second he finds primarily a creation of a separated church. His view is that much of the theology is unwarranted, invalid argument, not justified by the abuses.

There is a kind of subtlety in all of this. We began this essay by noting that Adam claimed that theological difference described accurately the causes for a divided church. But his argument seems almost to deny this. However, therein is the subtlety. Luther was not, according to Adam, as violently anti-Catholic, or at least against Catholic theology, as he was against the abuses of medieval church life. But the Lutheran church, in order to sustain itself against those abuses, developed a theology which argues the separation as a necessary one. Adam believes this churchly theology to be mistaken, just as the late Middle Ages church was mistaken ethically in not correcting the abuses before it was too late. For Adam, therefore, the reunion of Christendom is dependent upon the correction of ethico-religious abusive practices on the part of Catholics and the abnegation of mistaken theology on the part of Protestants. Luther is a source of both corrections, as he reads him.

Needless to say this is an interpretation of Luther a little alien to Protestant traditions. Whether right or wrong, there is a compassion in Adam that is clearly born of the spirit of Jesus Christ. It must be the better part of ecumenicity that allows men to write as he does, and we can only hope that Protestants will seek as arduously for unity with Catholics as he has apparently done from his side.

The concessions demanded by Karl Adam as the necessary condition for the reunion of Christendom are at once less in number than most people might assume and yet more demanding of the pride and convictions of sundry parties than can be reasonably expected. This is perhaps why even Leibnitz said three hundred years ago that reunion could happen only with "divine grace in abundance."

IV

It augurs well for contemporary discussions about the reunion of Christendom that there are voices like that of Karl Adam. For amid the decriers of the power of theological ideas and those who believe other non-theological bonds will be decisive, there are those who see theological expressions to be intimate expressions of religious faith. Theology is both an expression of faith and the occasion for it. It is true that theological rubrics are part of the intellectual coinage, but they can become truly evangelical when they are so used as to cause a man to intensify his passion and to deepen the furrows of faith in his life. It would be a shame if further ecumenical discussions should neglect this function altogether.

It is true, too, that theology can be misused. Theology can become a tool for the furtherance of non-religious ends. If I understand the charges Adam and others have levelled against the theology of the post-Reformation period, it is briefly that theology became a polemical device, a means to strengthen the claims of one institution against another. Whether this judgment is true about sixteenth and seventeenth century Protestant thought is a moot point. But, it is well to be appraised of the possibility. Much of the theology which became an argument seems at this date to be modelled after an inappropriate pattern, alien to religious uses altogether. For this reason, it is well to define the role of theology in ecumenical discussion once again. Contemporary churches need to guard themselves against misusing theology, even for noble ecumenical ends, as much as Protestants and Catholics did misuse it in centuries past.

The revival of theology in our day means the awakening of this peculiarly religious function. Those scholars who have shown us anew what theology meant to Luther, to Augustine, to Calvin, and to others, have also made clear to us that theology is not simply a tissue of argument. For a long while, theology seemed most glorious if it were an argument for God's existence or a defense of a position. Now we are beginning to see, with the help of detailed scholarship, that something was lost in such a turn of affairs. Luther, Calvin, Aquinas, Augustine and others have become truly ecumenical figures in their own right.

Something like this has also occurred in Biblical studies. Contrary to other times, when the Bible was treated as though it were the source of argumentative claims, we have also been taught to view it as a variety of religious expressions, though none the poorer for that. We are not as easily persuaded that the Bible is a series of premises or a congeries of implicit data, demanding a resolute reconstruction before its meanings can be made explicit. The Bible has become the possession of all Christians, in major part because of what the scientific scholars have shown us about it.

It is heartening, too, to note that the reunion of Christendom can even be broached by reference to theological views. There was a time, not too long distant, when the learned seemed to have reflected their way out of theology, not into it. Once there was a consuming skepticism among the learned that bespoke a despair about the possibility of theological agreement. Now this seems to have changed, for we are seeing exactly what theology is and what it does. There are rules for its promulgation and antecedents for its occurrence. The deepening of scholarship about the Bible, about the Reformation, and about numerous high points in devotion and theology have made these things clear.

Those churches which have lost all relation to theological traditions have lost too much. Once it seemed fashionable to insist that faith was ethical and not theological, or passional and not reflective, or attitudinal and not cognitive; and some Protestant groups so emphasized experience of a religious kind that theology became almost an embarrassment. Certainly the polemics of religion were dismaying, but to discard the tools of the polemics was also to discard one of the greatest means of grace, words themselves. The reunion of Christian churches demands a retracing of the works of God among us and, correspondingly, a re-evaluation of the language of faith.

CHAPTER TEN

Ontology and Faith: Paul Tillich

It is not often that extravagant things are said in public journals about a theologian. But our subject for this essay, Paul Tillich, is an infrequent theologian. He has been featured on a national television program, he has made *Life* and *Time*, he has been a Gifford lecturer. After leaving Germany under duress during the Nazi period, he graced the faculty of Union Theological Seminary in New York City for twenty years. Upon retirement he accepted a position at Harvard, which post he now holds.

Tillich's literature is rather many-sided. He has written some sermons which are tenderly evocative, almost plaintively invitational, to the new creaturehood which he discerns as the Christian right. On the other hand, he has written some very contrived and abstract argumentation too, some of it growing out of concern with particular religious matters, some of it stemming from questions that are traditionally thought to be philosophical. But all of his books are still of a piece. They are actually more irenic and pacific than they initially appear. For Tillich indeed writes out, either in sermons or treatises, a vast and commodious intellectual context in which almost everything gets some kind of place. His reflection has all kinds of appeal for the man who wants order and inclusiveness together. Unlike so many theologians and religious thinkers, who get order by excluding a variety of phenomena or who include the variety only by getting eclectic and encyclopedic, Tillich orders and includes almost everything. In one way, it must be admitted, he succeeds; but it is really by moving up to another level of abstraction, and this level, characterized by words like "being," "non-being," "estrangement" and others, is what makes it possible for Tillich to develop, as he says, a theological system for our period. He is a little sensitive about the criticisms which he has suffered on this score, to wit:

> But I cannot accept criticism as valuable which merely insinuates that I have surrendered the substance of the Christian message because I have used a terminology which consciously deviates from the biblical or ecclesiastical language.[1]

Tillich creates a new vocabulary for the theologians and the philosophers of our day. His system takes the familiar concerns expressed in the Bible and in earlier theologies, creeds, and confessions, and rewrites them in another language. By so doing the more mundane efforts of the philosophers are also said to be joined. It must be admitted that not as many philosophers are convinced of the validity of this effort as are theologians. The resulting tissue of words, wonderfully supple and spread over both theological and philosophical landscapes, looks like a new and different kind of summary of abstract learning. St. Thomas Aquinas wrote a *Summa Theologica* which was just that, a summary of theology. He supplemented this work with another big one, a *Summa Contra Gentiles,* which turned out to be a kind of summary of philosophy. Paul Tillich

---

[1]*Systematic Theology,* Vol. II (Chicago: University of Chicago Press, 1957), p.viii.

has been likened to a Protestant St. Thomas. But his work is quite different, for where Thomas divided revelation from reason and the works of a faith-inspired reflection from the works of unaided reflection, Tillich has put them together. Whether this is an effective and genuinely significant rapprochment awaits the patient and painstaking judgment of scholars. To this date, the magnitude and the novelty of the effort seem to have been enough to gain attention and to offer a few new points of departure.

Coming to America from Germany as a refugee in 1933, Paul Tillich has very often been in polemical relations to dominating trends of thought. In the developing days of German Nazism, Tillich was resolutely socialist in his politics. When theologians were espousing liberal religion and praising the potentialities of our common human nature, Tillich was their earnest critic and foe. When religious leadership became more conservative by reclaiming the Protestant Reformers and the work of Karl Barth, the Swiss theologian, Tillich urged a more sympathetic understanding of our secular life and learning. Now when the philosophers are scrutinizing language and its uses, Tillich urges the merits of ontology; and when existentialism threatens to become a new rage and another kind of non-systematic anti-intellectualism, Tillich is busy writing a large systematic theology.

II

However, this is not to say that Paul Tillich is cantankerous and obnoxiously different. He is really an irenic thinker, trying to bring together the strands of relevant thought in some kind of theological grasp. At the same time, he is seeking to restore the many persons of our time, who feel that words like "salvation," "sin," and "eternal life" are meaningless, to a lively and first-person understanding of religious matters. He tries to do this in a richly charged learned language. Granted that what may be Mr. Tillich's strength is also his weakness, still it is true that as a philosopher-theologian he uses metaphysical and ontological language, not only to aid the understanding, but also to stir the emotions and volition of his hearers and readers. Rather than that circumspect obeisance to rules, characteristic of most intellectuals, whose abstractions must be devoid of wishful and passional appeal, Tillich lets every abstraction be charged with emotion. His philosophizing and theologizing are done with a supposition alien to our time, viz., that if one speaks or writes most adequately, then that language will occasion volitional, emotional, and intellectual responses. Besides all of this, it will then be most religious.

Tillich is an expert in two different areas of communication. On the one side he speaks to those who are interested in the most abstruse and detached of intellectual-religious problems. He does this well, although there are difficulties of understanding replete on every page. But, on the other side, Tillich is also an excellent preacher. He speaks with great pathos and stirs his audiences, not by tricks of rhetoric, but rather by the enormous passion which flows through his often technical discourse. His writings and his speaking do not divide easily, because in the middle of abstract reflection of the highest order he is apt to let a pointed homiletic barb find its mark. Likewise, in the middle of a sermon, he is inclined to lead his audience in somewhat tortuous intellectual turns for the sake of his major point. Such abilities may be Tillich's weakness as a thinker, for sometimes he persuades where he ought to argue and argues where he ought to persuade, but such characteristics also account for the wideness of his appeal.

Anyone either having read this far or having read the technical religious literature of our day cannot help but note that there are major divisive problems facing the scholars and theologians. While religion is indeed on the upsurge socially, there are marked difficulties restraining enthusiasm among the intellectuals. Rudolf Bultmann's assertion that religious thought is shot full of mythology is a case in point. In this somewhat fractured intellectual context, Paul Tillich offers some healing with words. His suggestion is that there is no wide breach between Biblical religion, Jewish and Christian, and the language of "what is." Whatever the charge—that the Bible is folk-tales, myth, or bad science, or contrariwise, that philosophy and learning about "what is" are prideful self-assertion and only a tissue of self-protective claims—Tillich is certain that the parties are in error. The conflict between science and religion, between culture and Christ, between reason and faith, between the Bible and secular learning—these conflicts (for surely they seem plural) Tillich wishes to resolve. He tells us that ontology, the science of being, of "what is," is the answer. Even though Paul Tillich is a Protestant and believes that the assumption of finality and authority, spiritual or otherwise, is a sign of sin, still he is surely very close to the spirit of the natural theologians, who believed that reflection on "what is" might provide a clue to God.

Tillich, as has been noted, is often said to be the Thomas Aquinas of our century. Thomas, who is, even after seven centuries, the single most widely acknowledged theologian and philosopher of the Roman Catholic Church, wrote several compendia of Christian theology. He wrote summaries in which he argued the case for Catholic faith against some of the learning and all of the ignorance of his century. Paul Tillich is, indeed, a kind of Protestant Thomas but with some marked differences. He has the same yearning surely as the classical theologians, namely, to bring theology back into discussion with every appropriate field of learning. But in order to do that today, Tillich has to do what Thomas did not—vindicate the right of philosophy and theology to such a pretentious task. No longer is it agreed upon by the intelligentsia that the existence of God can be inferred from the characteristics of nature or even from the texture of human history. Philosophy and theology work, therefore, and in contrast to Thomas' view of the matter, within highly restricted areas of learning, in areas where the rules of warranted inference are well established.[2]

Tillich knows full well that the critical and restrictive character of scientific hypotheses is not a fortuitous matter. In fact he tells us, if we do not already know it, just why it is the case, even from the point of view of the sciences, that the skeptical attitude must obtain. God is hidden to cognition, and God is indeed the *deus absconditus*, the hidden God, as the Protestant reformers had insisted. So, if this be true, what then can be done by a theologian or a philosopher? Unlike Thomas, Tillich does not feel it intellectually proper to infer God's existence and nature from the given world. Tillich cannot summarize the world's lore on God's behalf. Therefore, he has to find another out. He believes he has discovered it, along with Kierkegaard and others, in the relatively unexplored question of "what it means to be." This is a root question, a radical issue, one that seems like the introduction to more serious thought. Tillich, however, believes that this science, and it is a kind of learning operating according to rules, enables its students to speak about all that is, not superficially and trivially, but with relevance and concreteness. The new *summa* is, therefore, being written in a new spirit; it is in its way critical, abstract, and yet supposedly related to the human condition. Besides, Tillich has convinced

---

[2]Most of these points can be read about in Tillich's *The Protestant Era* (Chicago: Univ. of Chicago Press, 1948), pp. ix-xxix; also Part II, pp. 55-114.

a good number of people that his effort is on God's behalf.[3]

III

Tillich holds that philosophy is the search for "ultimate reality." This he says not because the philosophers have told him to say it; for he knows how far the currents of thought have moved the philosophers, and, too, he has listened to them for twenty-odd years in America. Still, he insists that philosophy is not properly a discipline restricted to the technical problems of logic and epistemology. He finds this latter movement an aberration.

This means that Tillich is once again in opposition. For, on no point does there seem to be any wider agreement among a learned group than on the view that philosophy is a technical and analytic inquiry into the problems of the forms of thought, language and inference. Philosophers today chorus their disapproval of those who make suggestions, who sponsor doctrines, who advocate causes, who suggest that the content of learning can be increased by philosophizing itself. With spasms of modesty, the philosophers insist that clarity is their aim, that they are not provident of wisdom, but only the conveyors of a knowing about knowing, adding, as it were, only to the awareness about our awareness, and not to our knowledge of the world. All of this Tillich eschews as policy for himself. When others are analytic, he chooses to be synthetic; if others are interested in the abnegation of metaphysics, he cares about being; when others are critical, he is doggedly speculative.

Instead of arguing that the modern turn of affairs is an achievement warranted by the historical development of various issues, Tillich insists, from his own survey of the history of reflection, that philosophy is legitimately "that cognitive en-

[3]Tillich's *Systematic Theology* is currently appearing in five volumes, of which the first two are already published (Univ. of Chicago Press, 1951 and 1957).

deavor in which the question of being is asked." To some philosophers this will seem as perverse as a scientist's reiteration of an old hypothesis in apparent disregard of later evidence and hypotheses. But Tillich is not perverse; and he is not convinced that what he has to say is subject to strictures that are so devastating. He has a wonderful sense of humor and contents himself with a definition of his philosophizing that accords with his own eminently successful communication. He is making sense to somebody. He denies that he speaks nonsense—he says it is philosophy. Philosophy is knowledge in answer to the question about "what it means to be." One can ask this question in respect to anything about which it is relevant to say that it is. Tillich tells us that this question "is the simplest, most profound, and absolutely inexhaustible question." The inquiry he calls "ontology," which means the word about being. Ontology is, to Tillich, the central concern of philosophy.[4]

Mr. Tillich does not wish to feed the misconception that ontology is a science specializing in trans-empirical realities, worlds beyond worlds, or that philosophers have special cognitive organs for repudiating the common-sense convictions of men. Philosophers are "speculative," but in a chastened sense. They are (as the root word *speculari* means) "speculative" when they "look at things." Philosophers do not create imagined worlds, nor do they deal in intellectual black magic. It is Mr. Tillich's charge that modern philosophers are too selective in their attention, that they have forsaken what is, or at least much of what is. Ontological study is the acknowledgment of what is, and this acknowledgment and the consequent description of the structure in whatever is, means, in turn, that history, knowledge, values and nature are brought into view. Men cannot be men, Tillich insists, without asking questions about

[4]Note here Tillich's *Biblical Religion and the Search for Ultimate Reality* (Univ. of Chicago, 1955), esp. "The Meaning of Philosophy," etc. pp. 5-21.

being. Every man philosophizes just as every man moralizes and behaves politically. Some men do it with myths and epics, others in drama and poetry, but philosophers make the questions conscious and elaborate them methodologically. And philosophy is hand and glove, he argues, to the very structure and vocabulary of any language, including the language of religion.

Tillich is at pains, therefore, to show the normalcy of the question of being. For the question turns out to be several questions. We ask about the being of things, the being of ourselves, of the future, of ideas, even of the past. Each of these requires a separate ordering of concept and interest. Tillich is interested in isolating those features of being which occasion our knowing that we ought to speak and to write differently of the past than we do of the future, of imagined things as over against those which are actual. Unlike contemporary philosophers, who are alerted seemingly only to the differences between the languages and/or the ways of knowing, Tillich is alerted particularly to the modes of being, to the power and capacity of things and ourselves, which make kinds of language so pronouncedly distinct.[5]

Tillich is very certain that there is a generic problem of being. This is, so to speak, a natural problem, indigenous to people. The folk literature, the tawdry intellectual stuff of everyday life, and the sophisticated expressions of most refined cultivation give testimony to the presence and scope of the ontological concern. Therefore, this problem is not introduced by the philosopher or the theologian. The problem is already with men and only needs expression and a resolution.

So convinced is Tillich of the genuineness of the ontolo-

---

[5]This is the point made circumspectly in lectures published under the title, *Love, Power and Justice.*

gical problem and so impressed is he with ontological truths
that he dares to make ontology the court of meaning and the
interpreter of almost all of human speech and effort. For, it
turns out that hardly anyone can say all that he means. Every
bit of speech is a kind of fragment needing an interpretation,
almost a translation. It seems that no one can do justice to all
the meaning that there is unless he knows something of the
hidden quest and the presently unrevealed fulfillment. Ontology
clues one in on both; hence it becomes the locus by which human questing and satisfaction can be, in a measure, understood.

This is certainly an odd state of affairs. Just as psychoanalysts have proposed knowing about motivation better than
the agent himself, so Tillich, taking seriously the panoply of
talk and conviction about meaning, proposes an access to another's speech which the speaker or writer does not know. Ontology gives up its secrets only under duress, as is altogether
proper. Once the secrets are known, then all kinds of things are
understood anew. Modern art, Biblical theology, contemporary
philosophy, the Reformation, existentialism, and even science
come to mean something different than their practitioners believed.

IV

However, though the generating point of interest for Tillich's concern and the average man's may be the same, it simply
is not true that the upshot is. Tillich's ontology turns out to be an
extended essay away from the ordinary ways of speaking, even
the ordinary ways of theologians. So, for example, we are told
that to say that God exists is to deny Him.[6] God does not
"exist," because He is "beyond" existence. Putting the matter
in another way, the term existence simply cannot be applied to
God at all. Its inappropriateness lies in the fact that God is

[6]*Systematic Theology*, Vol. I (University of Chicago Press, 1951), p. 205.

"being-itself," beyond the range of the kind of term which we use for objects, for ideas and even for ghosts.

The science of ontology is not then quite about the "what is" that most sensible people understand and know. Though there is rather widespread lip-service to the search for reality, Tillich has little touch with the ordinary varieties of such inquiries. Most people who are looking for ultimate realities are favorably disposed to examine the cosmos itself. They try to surmise what is at the end of the causal regression, the first cause, or they speculate about some vast purpose that holds all the rest of the things in the world together. Even if men become sophisticated today, philosophical about reality, they still do not illustrate Tillich's kind of ontological inquiry. Looking for God somewhere in the cosmos and seeking Him as though He might answer the anxious quest for His being and existence—these are errors of great moment. However far such inquiries might be from the concerns of an ordinary man who wonders a bit, both are remote from Tillich's ontology. For he separates an ontological approach from what he calls the cosmological.[7]

"Man," we are told, "occupies a pre-eminent position in ontology, not as an outstanding object among other objects, but as that being who asks the ontological question and in whose self-awareness the ontological answer can be found."[8] If one looks around the cosmos, one tends to itemize and to describe things one sees. If one claims finally to find God somewhere in the vast cosmological reaches, God, in virtue of the kind of inquiry if nothing else, becomes another item in existence. Then we can use words like "exist" and "being" for God too. For such words seem appropriate for what is in the cosmos. Even

[7]The Theology of Culture (New York: Oxford Univ. Press, 1959), pp. 10-11.
[8]Systematic Theology, Vol. I, p. 168.

if God is invisible and His presence has to be inferred, still it is Tillich's point that God, when found by cosmological inquiry is but one more, though exceedingly important, item in the hierarchy or order or arrangement of being. And "being" is the word we use to designate in the most general way the minimal fact of existence.

Ordinarily ontology is understood to be the science which tries to tell people what exists. But Tillich is clearly on the side of telling us that what he means by an ontological inquiry is far indeed from inferring the unseen from the seen, far from conjecturing the nature of the first cause from secondary causes, far even from discerning the hidden features and perhaps unifying laws of the physical universe. Instead, ontology is engendered not by curiosity, not by the ordinary desires to know, but rather, by a very intimate and personal self-awareness. Men are deeply anxious, strangely absented from their goals, their fulfillment, their actual and desired selfhood. Men are in Tillich's language "estranged," separated, cut-off, and they are not quite sure from what. Men, he tells us, are alienated, they feel like pilgrims and wanderers, they are neurotically concerned and dissociated.

The ontological question is an anguished cry of all men and every man. But it is a terribly refracted and inchoate cry. Mankind finds numerous substitutes for the direct ontological query, sometimes the quest for beauty, sometimes the pursuit of cognitive truth, sometimes the drive towards goodness and solidarity of men. Tillich's point is that numerous intellectual, esthetic and moral pursuits, which promise "verum," "bonum" and "pulchrum" (truth, goodness and beauty), can and do disguise the simple little fact that men are estranged from the ground of their own being. Literally, Tillich wants to say, men are not grounded, they are not rooted and planted; they are not safe and secure, as one of Gospel hymns says "from all alarms." The ontological question takes shape only slowly, when self-awareness grows and the thought of a person dares to turn inward. Instead of the cosmos revealing anything healing, it is the torment within from which comes the initial impulse in the right direction.

Apparently Tillich's ontological question comes out of the "dimension of depth" which is every man's to explore and know. Even religion and not least theology can deceive a person. For much of the religious language causes men to believe, first, that there is a divine being somewhere in existence, and second, that religion is a rather special way of both knowing and otherwise relating oneself to such a being. The kind of theology and ontology which tells one about the divine being in such a manner is terribly vulnerable. Tillich tells us what is wrong when he notes:

> A God about whose existence or non-existence you can argue is a thing beside others within the universe of existing things. And the question is quite justified whether such a thing does exist, and the answer is equally justified that it does not exist.[9]

Both the atheistic scientists who believe that they have refuted religion when they rightfully show that there is no evidence for the assumption that such a being exists and the theologians who make God the highest being among other beings who, nonetheless, has given people information about Himself, both, Tillich concludes, are mistaken.

The word "God" ought to be reserved in Tillich's view for what is ultimate, infinite, and absolutely unconditional in man's spiritual life. And this is discovered when we turn inward and realize that our existence is tortured by a well-nigh

[9]*Theology of Culture*, p. 5.

inexpressible yearning and concern, an insatiable quest for meaning, order, and the very ground of the life we already live. Following a clue of Albert Einstein, who said that the true scientist "attains that humble attitude of mind towards the grandeur of reason incarnate in existence, which, in its profoundest depths, is inaccessible to man,"[10] Tillich tells us that there are numerous testimonies to the ground of all being of the physical world and suprapersonal values. This is the divine depth which is indeed inaccessible to words and ideas, to concepts and percepts. This is the ontological reality which is beyond rational discernment and scientific description.

When religious men use the word, "God," or the two words, "personal God," for such a ground of being, they speak only symbolically. "Symbolically" here means that they cannot speak literally as they would if God were another being among beings. For God is not an object, not a part of what is; He is spoken of as a person in order to do justice to the fact that the immediate relation to this ground of being is really an overcoming of one's estrangement. Religion is like being grasped by "the inaccessible ground and abyss of being," almost like being grasped by a person who saves you, who heals you, who puts you once again at rest after a nightmare of anxiety.

The ontological question then turns out to be rather different. Tillich is convinced that the language of Christian faith, of theologians and doctors of the Church, can be correlated with the ontological question. This in fact is what he explicitly says in a popular book on this subject to which we shall now allude.

V

Tillich fortunately has written a small book about this. It is called *Biblical Religion and the Search for Ultimate Reality.*

---

[10]Einstein quoted in Tillich, "Service and Theology: A Discussion with Einstein," *Theology of Culture*, p. 130.

The thesis of this bargain and summary is that the Bible is a record of the manifestation to various people, in "concrete, physical, and historical reality," of the divine. Biblical religion is a characteristic way of responding to what is thought to be the presence of God and a religious way of behaving in specific circumstances. The Old and New Testaments are about the manifestation of being, a divine being which is really the ground of being, to people who are religious. In so far as their religion, their worship, prayer and faith, become oriented to that numinous revelation, they share an identifiable Biblical religion.

The principal connection between ontology and the Bible story can now be seen emerging. For, after all the intellectual dust has settled, it turns out that the Bible is an account of "how" men have "to be." The way of man's existing, the story of what is involved in being a person, is told us in Scripture. Tillich is a theologian, not via nature and history, but via being. And here too, for him, is the nub of the contemporary movement called "existentialism." Tillich is convinced that having an ultimate concern about these matters is a distinctive and ennobling human characteristic. To be human you have to have concern—to be without concern is to lose your distinctiveness. Having an ultimate concern is what Tillich says Biblical faith is. Therefore, the tissue keeps getting thicker. The science of ontology shows us that being human is different from being natural or being ideal or being non-temporal. Ontology to Tillich enriches the understanding of theology considerably, so considerably, according to many of our learned contemporaries, that this man's thought is a new departure for Protestant thought.

Mr. Tillich is very adept at tracing the peculiarities of being human. He has done so at considerable length and in numerous interesting ways. What does it mean to be human? Tillich finds this a legitimate question. He knows that the change can be rung on "means" and "meaning." He finds it "meaningful" to say that to be human is to be concerned about one's own existence, one's qualities, one's structure and character, one's relations to all else that is. But is everything in flux? Is everything "which is" only transitional, temporary, passing? Is everything to be no more? Are all of our relations only transitional and temporary? Is there no permanence in "what is," no abiding place, no "reality" which is non-temporal, nothing which resists the urge to go on into nothingness and non-being?

Paul Tillich is a man of big words. He is daring the view that men are not quite without witness. He claims that the philosophers can be guided by the passion called by Plato the "eros for the Idea," "desire for wisdom" by the Stoics, "longing for truth" by Augustine, "intellectual love" by Spinoza, "passion for the Absolute" by Hegel, and "liberty from prejudice" by Hume. These driving enthusiasms, uniting passion and rationality, unite also the philosophers and their questions. The thinkers' existences becomes involved in their questions. Such philosophers produced ontological philosophy which does overlap with religion. It is not the quantity of philosophy or learning which overlaps; it is the quality. At the very least, he asserts, Biblical religion overlaps and answers the search for ultimate reality and being. This, an extravagant claim to be sure, is both cause and perhaps effect of the current widespread interest in matters of Tillich's kind of theology.

Whatever the judgment of the ages on Paul Tillich, he at least has tried to bring unity and order to our cultural life. Tillich has a passion for God and the social reconstruction of our strife-ridden society. He sincerely believes, and flatters all of the rest of us thereby, that the intellect must be renewed first of all. This is what he is trying to do. Perhaps only God can say whether this is the same grace as works through Christ reconciling the world unto God. Short of such an astounding disclosure, an obstreperous puzzle remains. It is to this that we turn.

VI

Tillich would have us believe something very odd about the language we speak. It seems that none of us ever can say all that he means. Or, to put it less queerly, everything we say means either something different or something more than we say. Therefore, it is altogether proper for a man to say something and then stop, and say: "Now what did that mean?" Tillich has split speech and meanings. Therefore, the quest for meanings is a special and extraordinary quest. It is almost as if no one can explain himself, for no one quite knows what he means. Not even honesty and a careful use of language is a sufficient safeguard, and knowing one's subject is not as crucial as knowing oneself.

It is difficult to know just where the mistake is in all of this. Certainly there are confusions of all kinds here, not least about what meanings in fact are. Also, Tillich seems to have been misled by the fact that many people ask about the meaning of this or that into thinking that their question is a real one and has an answer. So, too, with the problem of being. Because of a variety of ways of talking about things, Tillich allows a generalization about being to stand forth as the penultimate intellectual issue. It may well be that he is misled simply by the form of language itself. But, these technical issues need another and more serious treatment, and here it will be enough to make a brief rejoinder on more proximate considerations. For certainly Christain faith provides its own criticism of this kind of interpretation.

Is it not absurd to believe that Paul did not know what he meant? Is it plausible to believe that the New Testament needs an interpretation? According to Tillich, there is no language spoken which does not need elucidation. But this means that the language about theology is really better than the theology. Ontological language is actually about every other kind of language. It is philosophy "par excellence," and it explains the language of esthetic joy, of scientific description, of religious fervor. But this is precisely to rob these forms of expression of their role. Each of these ways of speaking provides a kind of explanation and a system of judgments and evaluations. But Tillich would have them all to be wanting; all of them are in need of a better orientation and a further reference.

If Christian faith makes any sense at all, it certainly makes it by drawing our attention to a condition that is universal among us and needs a remedy. Christian theology defines this condition as our sin and suggests that God is our Redeemer and Savior. Therefore, the language of faith declares that no one can escape this God and that all things under heaven are subject to His purposes. Tillich seems to agree with this view of the matter, but he only seems to agree; for this kind of view is again subject to an interpretation. All of us know that such a view is not easy for all people to understand. The lack of understanding has never demanded an ontological explanation. According to Christian theology and the Bible, understanding comes with putting oneself more securely in the moral context that the Bible describes, not in a still more abstract and general kind of inquiry. Tillich denigrates the religious life and the particulars of a man's existence by insisting that the court of appeal, even for faith, is ontology.

Thus it would appear that Tillich's theology is not really the language of faith at all. It is about faith and about theology.

It is the language of a very involved curiosity, led by the confused notion that everything is all right except that the meanings are missing. Because they are missing, one must philosophize about "being" to supplement the spiritual fare. It is no wonder that ordinary believers should be a bit mystified, but it is greater wonder that so many erstwhile scholarly and critical theologians should have been persuaded.

CHAPTER ELEVEN

The Bible and Theology: H. H. Rowley

There are almost countless ways to assess the importance of the contemporary literature, scholarly and popular, devoted to religious subjects. However, scholarship about the Bible has been rather insistent, in the last few decades, upon the theme that the Bible is a theological book. This is as much as to say that the Bible must be studied as though its language were religious. For a long while, when fervor was running high for assessing the Scripture historically, sociologically, and a variety of other detached ways, it seemed that technical study could admit anything but the fact that the Bible was intrinsically religious. It was left for preachers to discover the religious aspects, and if not the preachers, then the laymen and the devotional inquirer but certainly not the scholar. This state of affairs has changed radically in recent decades; and once again we are witnesses to a resurgence of Scriptural study, much of it posited upon the notion that unless the Scripture be studied as a religious piece of writing, its abiding significances for the life of faith and church will surely be lost.

Americans have been typically light on Biblical studies and so-called Biblical theology. Religious scholarship in this country has often focused on philosophical, psychological, sociological studies and has been strikingly empirical and experiential in concern. European universities have always kept historical, linguistic, and Biblical disciplines foremost. Within the latter, theology has had most of its dramatic fortunes; and it seems that the fortune of theology is waxing active again today, and again it is related intimately to these disciplines. Americans are turning today to historical and systematic theology, and also, to Biblical studies. Some critics of this tendency view it skeptically as a regression to things left behind in Europe, but the matter is more fundamental and serious than that.

The kind of religion which Americans call "liberal Protestantism" has illustrated quite well in the first half of this century the intellectual orientation and dependencies of our theologians. This kind of Protestantism defined itself as liberated from fundamentalist views, at least, those which claimed that the Scriptures were verbally inspired, disclosed a single system, and were together the single authority for religious experience and truth. In antithesis to this was a whole gamut of views, united perhaps by the methodological hope that critical studies on the Bible were altogether proper and that these, together with psychological, sociological, historical, and scientific studies of other subject matter, but notably man and his nature, might help us reconstruct a theology relevant to twentieth-century existence. American religion has always given expression to kinds of idealism and enveloping hopes for the future. When all these things were put together in a country burgeoning with economic opportunity and an almost rapacious exploitation of materials and talent, the effect religiously was an indigenous form of American Protestantism.

We have already noted in these pages the severe scrutiny

being given to the social forms that American religion has so naturally assumed. A corresponding scrutiny has also been accorded American Protestant theology. In some respects, the theological study has probably been less needed, because inadvertence and inattention here seem to affect fewer people. In any case, the kind of liberal theology, so long characteristic of American church life, has suffered several kinds of attacks. The optimistic views of human nature, supposedly grounded in scientific studies of man, have now been supplanted by views that are said to be more realistic, less hopeful perhaps, but more truthful. The doctrines of sin and of grace now seem more appropriate to man and his society, even as these are described by the disinterested scholars, than did the sanguine views once praised for their modernity. The Bible seems like a classic again, relevant and speaking to the universal conditions of men.

While it may not be a total sacrifice of dignity to admit that scholarship is also subject to whims, to fashions, and to pressures not always created by the requirements of knowledge, still it must be said that some of these current trends in religion are not popular only for such reasons. There is a notable example to the contrary. A view held by both American and European scholars of the past generation, namely, that the literature called "holy" by Christians and Jews, the Old and New Testaments, was a diversity almost as pluralistic in thought as it was in number of books, has been rejected and replaced because of detailed scholarship. I believe it fair to say that today the "diversity thesis" is rejected by men who are themselves of diverse systematic and religious persuasions and who believe that it is simply a mistaken way of describing that literature. Therefore, the point to remember is that the view is not rejected for abstract reasons alone or in most instances even principally; it is rejected because the view is misleading and deemed false on literary and descriptive grounds.

An excellent example of this shift in scholarly outlook is H. H. Rowley's Oxford lectures, *The Unity of the Bible*.[1] Professor Rowley is an internationally known Old Testament scholar, lately a professor at the University of Manchester. He is justly known for his twenty books, his discussion of the Dead Sea scrolls (published in 1951), his editing of *The Old Testament and Modern Study* (a compilation of essays by leading Old Testament scholars of the world), and almost countless articles in learned journals. Besides this, he has lectured in most of the famous universities of the world. By the industry of such scholars as Rowley, shifts in methods of study become both necessary and also well documented. Rowley's book on *The Unity of the Bible* is an overt declaration to the learned world that matters have changed in his field, and rather importantly.

Three questions will serve our inquiry: a) From what have Biblical scholars changed? b) To what have they changed? c) What is the significance of this change?

II

In response to the first question, it will be well to remember that not every scholar held the diversity view, and furthermore, that not every scholar who held what looks like this view held it for adequate reasons, or even for reasons like those disclosed by Rowley's comment. Individual instances have to be judged individually. But Rowley's contention is that when he was a young man in England it would have been "a hazardous thing" to announce a course of lectures on the unity of the Bible. As he says, such a title would have created the suspicion

---

[1]Published by Carey Kingsgate Press, Ltd., (London: 1953). Another treatment of this theme can be read in his *The Faith of Israel* (London, SCM Press: 1956), esp. "Introduction," pp. 13-23.

that the author was "an out-of-date obscurantist."[2] The emphasis instead was on the diversities. It was thought that the Old and New Testaments were as significantly different as vindictiveness and forgiveness are believed to be. Priestly religion was believed to be a large and unfortunate part of early history, redeemed only by the presence of a few rebellious prophets. The history of the literature was challenged, the poetry was approved. The morality was seen as evolving through a series of rather unfortunate historical developments. And likewise the New Testament was thought to be a rather helter-skelter collection of the theologies of Paul and other writers and the maxims of Jesus, disclosing a religion of confusing theology on the one hand, and of delightful simplicity on the other.

Perhaps it is not inappropriate to note that there were dozens of volumes doing what one did even in its title, i.e., proclaim the varieties of New Testament religion. What Professor Rowley does for Old Testament studies, Professor A. M. Hunter and several other scholars have done for New Testament studies, i.e., proclaim the end of the stress upon diversity and provide a new emphasis upon the unity.[3]

Rowley, like most of the Biblical scholars, is well aware of the genuine advances which nineteenth and twentieth century scholars brought to the field. They were right for criticizing that kind of unity given to the Old Testament by reading back into every passage the meanings of the New Testament. The skillful selection of compatible texts and an allegorizing of all the rest which were incompatible is another and artificial unity deservedly criticized. So here there is no overarching dogmatic unity being imposed again, with dis-

---

[2]*The Unity of the Bible*, pp. 1-3.
[3]*Ibid.* Professor A. M. Hunter's book is called *The Unity of the New Testament* (1943) and is only one of several such books on the New Testament.

regard for all the scientific study of the recent past. The point is, instead, that the scholars went too far. G. K. Chesterton, the English satirist, came to the conclusion after reading the Biblical critics that the five books of Moses were not written by Moses but by another fellow with the same name. C. H. Dodd, A. M. Hunter, and Rowley all tend to warn us away from the rather silly and sometimes absurd views that clustered around the Biblical field and which were given too wide a currency for what the evidence permitted. The view that the Bible is only a physical collection, not otherwise unified, is one of those views.

It seems, as one reads Mr. Rowley's book, that the unity of the Scriptures is not only a hypothesis which has been suggested by evidence, but is also a dispositional and a methodological guide for the working scholars in the field. For very complex reasons and partly, too, in sharp reaction to what must have seemed a too simple view of the unity of the Scriptures, the scholars were once inclined to treat the literature as if it were so differentiated in thought, in style, in authorship, and in historical origins that even its physical unity was something of a miracle. Rowley's thesis is that this disposition to stress the differentia is disappearing. He believes it has suffered attack because of all kinds of strenuous intellectual efforts to account for the facts. The flood of studies—minute descriptions concerning the origin and dating of the canonical books, studies of sacrifice, of the relation of law and the prophets, of ritual in Jewish and Christian circles—these and many, many more have produced new theoretical descriptions. The scholars exposed to these hypotheses in turn have increasingly found strengthened their disposition concerning the unity of the books.

III

This characteristic disposition, again not exclusively an hypothesis, but also an attitude ordering the scholars, fits the climate of opinion. It serves, too, as the answer to our second question: How has scholarship in this field changed? Rowley's answer is that the scholars are now inclined to stress the unity of the literature. They believe in the possibility of Biblical theology, which is as much as to say that despite the differences between books and authors, there is yet some kind of overlap and, furthermore, this overlap is describable. Without committing anyone to an apriori denial of development and of differences, Rowley still insists that there are all kinds of reasons for assuming that the convictions of Biblical peoples are remarkably similar, despite all kinds of differences in language, custom, and ethics, so that a theology, not several theologies, can state them.

The kind of unity Rowley describes quite clearly does not state, on historical grounds, the widespread belief that is an ingredient in most Christians' views, say, that the God of Abraham and Isaac and Jacob is the God of Jesus Christ. Many persons have held religious convictions to the effect that God began things, sustains them, had to do with Jews peculiarly, and had to do with Christians also in a special way in the person of Jesus. Rowley is a believer, if discernment is correct, in such matters. But such a conviction is not the kind he can claim is properly vindicated by historical and literary scholarship. There is a touch of modesty about Rowley in these matters, although an occasional religious enthusiasm can be detected here and there feeding his scholarship. He suggests that it is scientific in his field of learning to examine the faith as it is recorded and to examine also what people say in explanation of events and experiences. This is to admit only that men have

believed that they were witnessing or experiencing and record-
ing what to them was "the activity of God in human experience."

The Bible is, then, a record of what people have believed.
Just as Butterfield argued that God's ways were not open to
the technical historian, so, too, does Rowley argue that God's
ways are not open to the Biblical scholar. The unity of the
Bible is comparable to the unity that an individual acquires
in a lifetime. Something of character, of uniqueness, is developed increasingly over a long period of time. So too with the
Old Testament and the New. The diversities and tendencies are
eventually brought into a kind of dynamic unity, never a system, but rather into an open end process which has definite
teleological and purposeful aims.

Mr. Rowley is obscure on several points here and requires
both a close first-hand reading and some clarification of argument. I suppose him to be agreeing with what other scholars
have found is a discernible and empirically defineable kind of
believing common to Old and New Testament writers. Mr.
Rowley or no one else is saying that the writers' relation to
God is of the order of fact open to the historian. Still the belief
about the relation is impressive enough. Rowley says, too, that
scholars now are inclined to say that consequently there is a
"fundamental conception of the nature of religion which belongs to the whole Bible." In Mr. Rowley's words, this religion is "man's response to the achieved work of God, his yield-
ing to the constraint of grace, . . . the lifting of his life into the
purpose of God."[4] This is to admit that scholarship documents,
in this instance, human behavior and belief, not God's. But
some humans behave in peculiar ways when they believe in
God. Instead of the Bible being a collection of assorted pat-

[4]The above quotations are from Chapter I of *The Unity of the Bible.*

terns of human behavior, a kind of pot-pourri of this and that, it is through and through religious. Biblical figures believe in an identifiably religious way.

But to say this much still may seem rather piddling. An illustration may be in order. Scholars of other generations have been concerned to show that it is not easy to document the view that God caused equally Adam, the serpent, the Exodus, Mt. Sinai and the origin of the law, the Exile, and other wondrous events. On first glance, the Old Testament (and the New Testament too) relates all of these to God, and this seems to be all that can be said. Rowley is alert to the fact that each of these occurrences or persons can be otherwise described. That is, all kinds of other events and people might be discovered and known by what are, in some sense, contributory causes. For several generations this was the way of knowing and learning about such events. All of such learning seemed, too, to be an attack upon religion itself. Everyone was alert to differentiating the events by showing the natural etiology by which the events could be explained. Now it is as if many students have seen that the religious convictions of the Old and New Testament authors were not quite the sort to be either finally substantiated or finally refuted by scientific scholarship. Suddenly it has become clear that the Bible is a testimonial to or an account of a complex of beliefs. The Bible is not principally a book about nature and history—it is about people, their faith, and their God. Rowley states it something like this, that underlying the whole thought of the Bible is the idea of a God who reveals Himself in history and experience. And whether right or wrong, that idea is the making of a religion which puts Adam, Exodus, Law, Prophets, and Christ in a single matrix of beliefs. Whatever is otherwise true of Law or Christ, still the believer puts them together. The unity of the Bible is this complex of beliefs, and contemporary scholarship has both identified this unity and made the disposition admitting this useful for further scholarship. All the events can be otherwise known and differentiated, but the point of being religious is precisely to put to them together, to believe that in such ways God is revealing Himself. This is not to say that the beliefs are true or false; but at least such beliefs are the identifiable threads in the Bible.

IV

The last question is to ask ourselves how we state the significance of this change. One might suggest with some reason a certain caution about accepting the thesis that the Bible is a unity. Mr. Rowley certainly cautions his readers. The greatest care is necessary in defining what one means by that unity. Rowley knows what he means and he does not disregard the differences. But many others leap to the view that there is a unity in order to forget the differences. Furthermore, there is also a lesson in all this for every student, namely, to mind his dispositions. In the wish to help others to a freedom from limiting presuppositions, it may be that new ones, just as limiting, are created. It has become almost a fad today to lampoon the earlier scholars for what are assumed to be their excesses. Their greatest excess and error was to take too much for granted and to read out what they took for granted, as the conclusion to their inquiry. The thesis that the Bible is a unity, fortunately or unfortunately, goes together with the strong religious tide. It may be that excessive enthusiasm will again dispose men to see what is not there. But at the moment scholars of great learning and rather rare detachment are saying that the Old Testament and the New are more significantly a unity than they are a diversity. The thought can be treasured and used as the best that is permitted at this moment.

There is still another aspect. It is heartening to have scholarship and devotion, science and preaching, brought together to some extent, be it ever so slight. For the recovery of the notion that Biblical literature is the language of faith, a language of enthusiasm and conviction, puts Biblical studies back into the orbit of daily use and appropriation. The church in recent times has suffered too long from the cleft between technical study, on the one side, and religious affirmation, on the other, almost as if there were two truths, one for the scholar, another for the worshipper. Admitting still the logical difference between the language about the Bible and the language of the Bible, it is pertinent that this distinction be recognized by the scholars. It has meant that no longer are we expecting scholars to make a new theology for us or to constitute a new way of speaking about God for our generation.

On the other hand, the emphasis upon Biblical theology and the unity of the Scripture also has its difficulties. After all, the differences are still there to be reckoned with. The temptation is to disregard them or to explain them away. But there is still the possibility that the new kinds of scholarship will do again what was done in the past. By neglecting the differences and emphasizing some encompassing unity, we can create a theology which no single person in the past ever thought for himself. Likewise, such a theology might well prove to be the kind which no one could think for himself today either.

Modern Biblical studies are extraordinarily ambitious in our time. It is almost as if the care of the evangel has fallen to their hands. Consequently, an ambitious theology is sometimes proposed via the Scriptural science and study, which views its teaching as though it were fit not only for initiates but also the plain men. The anomalous situation arises that finds us insisting that the Scripture is the Word of God and, simultaneously, proferring a new Biblical theology as the essence of the matter. The plain man, unadorned by the equipment of academic life, is simply unable to share this universal and ambitious theology. Perhaps this circumstance accounts for the fact that so much of the current theological revival is popular on college campuses and only indirectly, if at all, among less sophisticated people.

If the modern study of the Bible is going to do something for the average man, the ordinary believer, which the Scripture can not do for itself, then we have an odd situation in the making. For if a man is to be saved by a technically achieved theology, he must be saved by one that he understands or by one that he does not understand. In the latter case, his theological thinking has to be done for him, apparently by a Biblical scholar. This seems a strange place for vicariousness. The scholar becomes the authority, and men are asked to believe in him; in the faith and language of the scholars about the Bible, men are saved. Certainly such a state of affairs is reprehensible because we seem to have such good authority for the dogma that the day of authority is past. More than this, any good scholar, like H. H. Rowley and other Biblical scholars, must feel uncomfortable. Doubtless it makes him glad to share insights with his fellow men, but it could scarcely occur to him, a Christian student, to ask for faith in the fruits of his scholarship.

However, there seems to me to be another conception of theology, less ambitious perhaps, but still related to every man and also to the Scripture. Theology here is understood to be both the expression of a need within an individual person and the expression of the satisfaction of that need in that person. Its assignment of significance is to a limited sphere in the lives of a limited number of people. Perhaps this is the way to understand the unity of the Bible too. Instead of that unity being trumpeted abroad in another vast theological system, perchance the Scripture, with its differences and qualities, is a symptom of a more fundamental likeness among men. Is there not a common need? Is there not a common Savior? Is it not also true that our faith teaches us that all men ought to be priests?

The primitively original expressions of faith in the Bible are, by themselves, more appealing to the rank and file of men than are the more trivial renditions of pedagogues and commentators. For the Apostles were not trying to be theologians in the technical sense of that term. They did not use theology to forget what it meant to be a man. In fact, it is almost as if their reflection was a means to their becoming Christians. So, we need to be reminded that the Bible is not a popularization of a more abstruse and unifying doctrine, nor is a theological system a distillation of amorphous and unreflective Biblical bits. And, a theological scheme, even purporting to be of the Bible, is no short cut to heaven. The way is still narrow. Theology grew very modestly in ancient times. It prospered in modest men, the men of the Bible, whose highest interests were spent upon realizing their new calling as children of God. What they did, we must also do. Our highest potentiality is declared to us in the Scripture. Nothing ought to gladden us so much as the fact that the Bible is again acknowledged to be of God, except that strange thought, namely, that we, each of us in turn, have to be of God ourselves, in affection, interest, enthusiasm, love and hope.

It would be another misuse of Scripture to treat it solely as the means for the realization of purely intellectual values. This is the temptation of modern rejuvenated religious scholarship. It is hoped instead that the unity of Scripture will be a token of the fundamental unity of all men before God.

CHAPTER TWELVE

Language, Theology and Faith

The best way to understand the Christian faith is by reading the Bible. This means that Christians are referred to words, even to a particular set of words, in order to answer their queries about faith. Certainly events and deeds make their point, but when they fail to clarify, there are always the words. The Bible is not only about the faith or even statements about the faith; rather, the Bible is a grouping of language-acts, not only language about acts. The language of the Bible has long been credited with power, and Christians have over and over again cited it with special attention to its power over the readers. Perchance that power is resident in the fact that the language of the Bible is replete with faith, with first-hand Christian living, so that every piece of language, or at least many of them, is a performance of an action. Professor Austin of Oxford University has noted that "I promise" is in itself the making of a promise and is not a mere statement about a promise. So, too, confessing that Jesus is Lord is a language-act.

Words are really very strange things. Though all of us use them continually, we are very hard put to it to explain the differences between their uses, the way in which they come to mean and to function for us, and how so many problems have arisen respecting them. An odd feature of ordinary life is the strange cynicism about words. The waggish paraphrase of Coleridge's famous line reads: "Words, words, everywhere, and not a thought to think." Other times it is said that words are empty; that they are idle, cheap, easy, impressive, meaningful, meaningless, precise, loud, and fatuous; and one of the mose devastating charges is to say simply that words are "just words." For, if men use words in a context which is void, if nothing has preceded them and nothing follows, then words alone are bound to fail. We speak regretfully of men when they talk too much, when they talk but do not mean it, when they talk, talk, and talk. All of this is as bad as not talking at all.

Almost everything human finds its way into our words. Lovers and learners must learn to talk and talk to learn. And most of the theories about language have been too limiting in scope to do well by the many-sidedness of speech. The satisfactions are multiple; for, we talk to communicate, we talk to express ourselves, we talk to make noise, we talk to stay busy, we talk because we must; we talk to show that we are alive, intelligent, religious, loyal, and sincere. Even if we do not talk, the written word has satisfactions too. How else can we explain those ignominious scraps of paper, secreted by solitary men, carefully attesting the tribulations of the spirit, albeit for no one's satisfaction but the writer's? To take a man's capacity to talk or to write is like removing the last vestige of his humanity. A book in hand, a pencil within reach, an uttered and meaningful sound—these have been the signs of hope and the marks of justice for tormented men, otherwise deprived of elemental freedoms.

Because language does so many things for us it also helps sometimes to deceive us. Thus, there are numerous ambiguities created by the fact that we do not know how we are supposed to take another man's words. Sometimes, the words are plain, but not knowing the speaker, we seem to miss all that he meant. Other times, by mistaking the use of a given word, we misinterpret an entire paragraph. Commonly we say that we hear the words, but that we do not know what meanings were or are intended. To hear the word seems a relatively simple psychological matter; but, to understand a given word provides most of the difficulties. Here we come upon something called the meaning, and meaning does not always obtrude itself like the physical word, whether written or spoken. Therefore, our ambiguities and confusions attendant upon language are said to be difficulties of getting the meanings clear.

There is, therefore, a peculiar plausibility to the common expression: "I heard you, but I don't know what you mean." For hearing, like reading, is often judged to be separable from understanding; and understanding is another process, rather internal and invisible, having to do with meanings, not just words. One might label all of this talk about talk, this view about language, a kind of metaphysics of language. Such a view does not even appear to be a surmise, a speculation, or a theory. It is written large in the convictions of learned people, almost as the silent accompaniment or adjunct of their proficient use of language. Many people use language, and very successfully too, without having any kind of surmise about how it works. But learned people, whose specialties often require the scrutiny of language, are quick to diagnose the troubles somewhere between the words and their meanings.

Our day has witnessed a peculiar shift of attention. For philosophers were often believed to be the experts on meanings. Philosophers were, and still are, arrogated to positions of high importance in the intellectual economy, and not least, because meaning looks to be their subject matter. Once it was almost as if meaning had its own locus, separate and distinct, access to which could be had only by the most strenuous reflection. Plato's dialogues have been a model for the learned in this very regard, for he suggested that there were "ideas," pure and undefiled, apart from the world of everyday things, which gave the truest and the richest meanings. Only the rare and aristocratically qualified thinker could know such ideas, and it was by reference to such thinkers that the rest of men would learn to conduct themselves properly. But the point moot to our discussion is that even the conduct of language got its rules in such intellection as the philosophers could manage. Plato's pages heap scorn upon the Sophists, who, among other dubious attributes, tend to study linguistic usage and spend inordinate effort upon teaching the art of rhetoric in vulgar disregard of the realm of ideas and their meanings.

There is, unfortunately, a long and solemn history of philosophizing in this manner. This attention has been unfortunate because it has hampered reflection rather than stimulated it. Realms of meanings, realms of ideas, realms of truth, beauty, and goodness, have beckoned countless intelligent people, almost like the Siren of Homer's pages. Instead of being a tool of reflective interest, such a theory has become the goal; and radical examination of the theory has invariably seemed a threat to the intellect, if not a sign of moral evil and irreligion. Everyone with enough imagination to look for meanings appears to have been compelled by the very conventions of the quest to seek them outside of the language, in some more refined stuff or in the structure of being itself.

But within the past thirty years or so, attention of many thinkers has been turned to language itself, the very language by which this supposed realm of meaning, being, and truth, has been posited and described. What looks like skepticism and debilitating introversion is that, to be sure; but it is also something more. It is also a continuation of the quest for meanings, with one major difference. Instead of looking through the language into something else, either the intentions of the speaker or the referents of the language, contemporaries are wont to look at the language itself, to see if another formulation is not possible. Professional philosophers are entangled in this kind of quest in our day. The outlines of problems are not very clear, nor are the solutions very compelling. Meaning is still the problem for most of the philosophers.

II

There are many issues compounded in the pages of the contemporary philosophy, despite the oft-made claim that analysis and positivism would dispell the multiplicity. For it may well be that another Socrates, clear headed and courageous, could convince us that if we thought clearly, there would be no problem at all. Wittgenstein, whose *Philosophical Investigations* have been recently been published (posthumously), tried not to give an answer to many philosophical questions, but rather tried to force attention to the genesis of the problems. If one saw how problems came to be, then he suggests one might learn that there is really no problem there at all. But to say this here is not to resolve anything for the reader, it is only to suggest that there is a ferment abroad respecting these matters. That ferment began on technical questions of meaning. Today the ferment has reached into other areas, including theology. The second section of this chapter will discuss briefly the so-called positivist theory of meaning and its effect upon the understanding of theological discourse. The third section will turn to a few additional issues relevant to our religious concerns.

Every religion has its language, if not its languages. Becoming religious is, in part, a matter of learning a new language. Gradually a man of faith learns how to give up the worldly tongue, that patois by which earthiness and vulgarity, the flesh and worldliness, are both expressed and encouraged. For there is another kind of speech; and, it is not an idle admonition, calculated for momentary effect, to wit, that our conversation ought to be in heaven. Religious speech is not only an index to its user, but it is also his guide and his deed. It is essential that we correct our language, as well as our direction and self estimate.

The language of faith has its diversities and kinds too, just as everyday living does. The Bible includes poetic pieces, hymns and choruses of emotional tenor, historical accounts, moral judgments, language in the past, present and future tenses, and language in the indicative and imperative moods. Recent Biblical scholarship has taken detailed notice of these kinds of linguistic usage; and today we are well advised to take seriously the proprieties and improprieties of poetry as over against prose, the passages which are descriptive as over against imaginative, and those which are historical rather than admonitory. There are good reasons for believing that poetry has a different use, different norms, and different things to say, than historical accounts. And, so too, with a variety of other styles and kinds of literary expression within the Holy Scriptures.

However, there is a long standing habit of intellectually oriented students of the Bible to interpret these many literary expressions as if they were non-literal and occasional endeavors to say what could be said less ambiguously and less confusing in a more straight-forward kind of prose. Doctrines often have been so couched as to be non-aesthetic in form, literal rather than suggestive, technical rather than conventional. It is, therefore, theology which has been often conceived as a science and made up of literal and somewhat idealized and artificial sentences, which conveys the truth of religion. Much of theology has looked like an artificial language, not itself Scriptural, but translated, as it were, out of the medley of kinds of language that Scripture is. Doctrines were not explicitly present in the Scripture, but it has seemed to many theologues that the meanings were there. It is as if the variety of languages, everything from Psalms to historical accounts, pointed to profound and overarching meanings. To state these meanings became an extra-Biblical task, a scholarly endeavor.

Words like "systematic" and "dogmatic" are more easily applied to theology, if one means by theology that highly refined and ordered translation, than they are to the Bible itself. Pascal notes this kind of problem in another context. In 1656, Professor Arnauld denied that a number of propositions attributed to Jansenius and condemned by the late pope could be discovered in the major book by Jansenius. Pascal came to Arnauld's defense in a most brilliant book, *The Provincial Letters.* His case is posited upon the rather simple fact that Arnauld's and Jansenius' decriers are everlastingly interpreting texts. They are so intent upon the meanings of the text that they finally overlook the text. Pascal, therewith, notes the same kind of distinction we have already alluded to, and he shows very penetratingly how his opponents' intellectual talents, not their absence, has caused them to invent something else by which to give substance to the text; and this something, the meanings, has really added to the text, not illuminated it.

It would surely be a mistake to conclude from this reflection that all theology was, by its very intent, false. Certainly it is appropriate to remember the distinction between language about religion and the language of religion. Theology, in fact, is the language of religion, and it is about God and His relations to the world and men. But, it behooves contemporary students of theology to keep their categories straight these days and to recover the variety of theological uses that Scripture provides. Not only does this promise justice to Christian and Jewish sources, but it also makes more sense of theology. For the kind of idealized sort of theology, highly refracted and systematic, has been subjected to devastating kinds of criticism, particularly from language-analysis philosophers.

Their point is simply made and grows out of reflection upon what makes factual and literal language meaningful. If all the truth of religion is stated in doctrinal and idealized language, which is both about matters of fact, i.e., empirical, and yet about a transcendent God, then it is not too difficult to show that such theology is meaningless. This is the point, then, of saying that theological language, if it claims to be literal, factual, and yet transcendent in reference, is simply nonsensical. Theologians might counter by saying that the philosophers are not the umpires and that they, the theologians, can play this game too. If rules are to be made up as one goes along, why can't theologians make them up as well as scientists or scientific philosophers? But this misses the point, perhaps the most crucial point. Whether the positivistic philosophers are right or not, the theologians have already perpetrated their difficulties by insisting that theology is like the sciences or other factual disciplines in being truthful, literal, empirical, or what have you.

This is not to say that theology is non-literal, only poetic, symbolic, or an expression of an attitude. This judgment is again wrong; for it assumes that the criteria for discussing and understanding theology are identical with the criteria for discussing other kinds of language, scientific and scholarly. Whether one says one thing or the other, affirmatively or negatively, the issue is wrong; for theological talk has to be studied as it is. If one studies the language of religion, as it is, and foregoes the pleasure of interpreting it immediately into something more meaningful, then the questions of meaning, of understanding, get another locus altogether.

The difficulty might be seen from a slightly different vantage point. If meaning is an objective referent for speech, then there ought to be criteria for determining when language fits and when it does not. If language becomes meaningful under some conditions and not all, then it becomes relevant to determine which conditions are the right ones, which the wrong. This is what the positivists have been trying to do. Their point, almost a metaphysical point, to be sure, is that meaning is not bound up with essences, with pure being, or the invisible structures of the world. Meaning, for them, is a linguistic matter. Meaning is clear and precise only when language is clarified and precise. Meaning is made by talk; it is not antecedent to language or independent of human acts. Against the traditional philosophers who seemed to believe that there might be levels of existence, or invisible worlds, or real ideas, by which meanings can be ascertained and adjudicated, the positivists have suggested that clear meanings are a function of clear language. So, like the theologians who have found most literary expressions unclear, so the positivists have found the everyday speech full of ambiguities. The clear speech and, hence, most meaningful, about the world and things therein is scientific speech, and not all of that.

A paradigm kind of speech or language is proposed then as the meaningful stuff, by comparison to which most forms of speech seem less meaningful if not nonsensical. In so far as theologians have proposed systematic theology as the paradigmatic kind of truthful speech, against which poetic and historical accounts seem only approximations, there is an analogy between theologians and the positivists. It is this analogical notion which has made positivism's attack upon theological assertions so pertinent. The philosophers have claimed that they now know the rules for the successful promulgation of factual truths. They seemed to believe, though not uniformly, that verification of a claim about matters of fact was a rule-like condition for speaking meaningfully. In any case, theological language, again of the highly contrived and systematic sort, not the less formalized language of the Bible, simply did not comply.

If theologians are stuck with the task of rendering the language of the Bible into something more meaningful, almost as if the original authors could not quite do what was necessary, then it behooves them to translate with all possible speed. And, if everything is in Scripture except the meaning, then scholarship is surely not a luxury; it is an absolute necessity. Then a further responsibility is in order, namely, to formulate very clearly the criterion for theological meaning; for it will not do to try to play the theological game with rules of another game. Theologians have, in fact, been thrown out of the game they wanted to play. Either they get out of the game or they play one of their own.

III

Other considerations have been forthcoming in the last decade or so. Books like *Essays in Philosophical Theology* and *Faith and Logic* are a symptom of change in the philosophical world. Once the major metaphysical questions seemed paramount; for reasoned conclusions about the nature of things, not just the agglomerations of observations and opinions, gave promise of serving a variety of interests at once. Questions about values and the standards of conduct, about knowledge of the world, and about God could all find their satisfaction in metaphysical theory. The particular form that God questions took in this context found resolution in something called philosophical theology. But, positivism, among other currents of thought, gave pause to such proceedings. It suggested that philosophy ought really to be refashioned along the lines of language analysis. If metaphysics is a profitless pursuit anyway, then another way to handle perennial questions must be found. That way was abstruse and difficult, more difficult certainly than old-fashioned metaphysics; for it meant that criteria for meaningfulness had to be isolated and stated. By and large, this meant the creation of another language altogether, a more ideal and refined speech, in which all the predicates of less precise ways of speaking might nonetheless be clearly set forth.

The task of philosophical theology takes, then, quite a different line. The books noted above, and many more besides, are in part examples of the new philosophical theology. But one might choose a theologian like Rudolf Bultmann as an illustration too. However, not all is at rest in the new philosophical Zion. Some disquieting tones have been struck recently. A few of these will be noted, first, among the philosophers, and, second, among the religious scholars of our time. And, the books already mentioned, edited by Anthony Flew and Basil Mitchell respectively, show the effects of the shifting views of the analytic philosophers, along with the debt to earlier positivism and its meaning criterion.

Suppose, for the moment, that meaning is not really something apart from words at all. Suppose that "meaning" is the word used to described the successful understanding and use of a word or words. Then one has a new way to comprehend the distinction between words and meanings. Ordinarily, learned people who make the distinction feel bound to treat meaning as if it were a something. Meaning seems to be a noun; it ostensibly names either that object of intention when you speak (then a distinction is drawn between intending and speaking) or another kind of ideal stuff or substance, perhaps non-intentional, by which words are accorded their abiding significance. All kinds of questions about the metaphysics of meaning have been raised. Positivism found the earlier metaphysics wrong, and in effect proposed another one altogether, linguistic and scientific-like, by which language could be vindicated and puzzles resolved. The new analytic philosophers are going a step further and asking questions about the distinction between meaning and language. In so far as there is any agreement at all, it seems to hover around the thought that the workings of the rest of language, the context of speech, the context of a particular word or sentence, gives the meanings. Therefore, what goes before and what comes after a word tells us what a word means. When we know how to use the word, we know what it means.

Of course, this is not, strictly speaking, another philosophical view at all. It does not answer the old question: "What is meaning?" To this date, however, it must be admitted that the newer philosophers continue to handle these proposals for action, namely observe the use, look at the context, try an example, as if they were more answers and better ones. Be that as it may, the contemporary gambit for the bright young men is to analyze, and most of them do it in satisfaction of the same quest for knowledge about whatever happens to concern them.

Most of these modern studies of theology, philosophical theology indeed, try to tell us what theology means. So, one man tries parables and suggests that all of the rest of the Biblical sayings have to be viewed with the parable-style in mind. Others tell us that theology is plainly enough in an indicative and present tense linguistic form, but that what is meant is something quite different. One gentleman, apparently simultaneously moved by religion to fervor and by philosophy to stringency, insists that these indicatives disguise imperatives. The stories are actually policy-proposals. Apparently most of the language of religion is an illy-contrived attempt to get some admonitions across. And so it goes. Whether anything substantial will come of all this is another matter altogether.

One would have thought that both contemporary theological and Biblical scholarship, on the one side, and some strands of reflection occurring in the pages of Wittgenstein, Kierkegaard, and Plato (especially those pages about Socrates), perhaps too some others among careful journeyman thinkers, on the other side, might have conspired to produce another posture on the part of those with such learned problems. I suspect that religious language does not need an interpretation at all. Most of it, at least the Biblical kind, is not highly technical. What is missing when we say that we do not understand it, is not something esoteric and rare, something to be apprehended by technical scholarship and tedious learning. Its meaning is to be found only when our context of action and speech makes it appropriate. If Biblical scholarship has made anything clear, it has shown how important the context really is. The Hebrew's questions were not mal-formed Greek questions; neither were the Hebrew answers barbarous and illogical by comparison with the Greeks. Their interests were different and their proposals duly appropriate. We owe a great debt for the clarification of understanding that numerous scholars have brought the rest of us here.

More particularly it seems that the language of faith has

been seen to be exactly what it is. Form criticism and all kinds of other textual studies of Old and New Testaments have shown us that the language was meant to be what it is. No one was, apparently, "really" trying to state a doctrine and then ended up by telling a parable or singing a Psalm. Religious literature was not a good try, a valiant effort, now to be understood by its consummation in another tissue of concepts.

And the philosophers might have surmised something like this too. For is it not the case that poetry does not gain meaning by being interpreted in prose? The way to understand poetry is to read it; then, read it again, again, and again. Some poetry may be nonsense and terrible poetry, just as some religious language might well be quite pointless. But the notion of a common referent for both, by which meaningfulness if not truth, could be encompassed appears downright gratuitous. Religious language does not need a translation into another idiom and neither does poetry.

Instead of looking for the meaning apart from the religious language, we ought to look for all the cues there are by which to put that religious language to our own use. We began by noting that the language of faith was not simply a piece of speech, an idle word play. Notably, the Scripture tells us to confess with our mouth that Jesus is Lord. Such a confession is the very performance of faith, not merely a sign of it. This is not all there is to faith, of course, but it is part of it. So to approach the language of religion as if it demanded an interpretation before its meanings could be apprehended, this is to miss its significance altogether. Religious language does not disguise another philosophy, and it does not get its warrant from an odd lot of presuppositions either.

There is a point, therefore, to learning how to read the Bible and other theological literature. Just as critics of modern poetry have taught us to read the poetry rather than everlastingly reading books about it, the author, and its historical setting, so, too, we have to learn to read the religious literature. There is no single way to do that. Though the debt of modern students of the Bible is great indeed to the countless scholars who have improved our knowledge about the Scripture, still this kind of knowledge is not a substitute nor even the necessary condition for reading the Bible as religious literature. The minimum essential for understanding the words as God's Word is the passion that faith also is, and, in addition, some awareness of the distinctive religious (principally Jewish and Christian) categories by which the authors are informed. One learns the latter most easily by exposure to all parts of the literature. Together, the passion and the categories, make the literature distinctively religious.

It remains to be seen whether modern linguistic philosophies will do adequately by the distinctiveness of religious language and meaning. To this hour, only the promise is there.

CHAPTER THIRTEEN

Mythology and Faith: Bultmann

Despite the strong aversion so many Americans express concerning the detachment and unrelenting intellectuality of so much of German theology—we like to insist that it is too academic, useless for the pulpiteering task, typically impractical —still the most remarkable and definitively influential books which have characterized theological developments in the last half century are aimed at the homiletical responsibilities of the preacher.[1] They are Adolf Harnack's *What is Christianity* (1900), Karl Barth's *Epistle to the Romans* (1919) and Rudolf Bultmann's essay (1942), the descriptive title of which ought to read, "The Problem of De-Mythologizing the Message of the New Testament." All of these books were written to help those men who guide the church. In the words of Karl Heim, another venerable German theologian (already cited in Chapter Five) : "The Church is like a ship on whose deck festivities are still kept up and glorious music is heard, while deep below the water-line a leak has been sprung and masses of water are pouring in, so that the vessel is settling hourly lower, though

---

[1]Erich Dinkler, "The Existential Interpretation of the New Testament," *Journal of Religion*, vol. 32, p. 86.

the pumps are manned day and night."[2] One might say on behalf of Harnack, Barth, and Bultmann, that all have written theology for the preachers. They have tried to remedy the fundamental weaknesses, the leaks in the ship as it were, by giving the weapons of repair to the preacher.[3] To forsake the metaphor, these theologians have found that preaching as a Christian communicative device has suffered from irrelevancy and for various reasons. Harnack used historical criticism to help the preacher recreate a religion of love, the religion of Jesus; Barth rejected historical criticism in order to isolate the *skandalon* of Jesus Christ; and now Bultmann, who has for almost a dozen years been the center of European Protestant discussion, has refurbished the critical and analytic tools for the negative purpose of demythologizing the New Testament, and the affirmative purpose of giving the preacher a pertinent and urgent message.

Bultmann takes a stand against the current Biblicism of European Protestantism, particularly the kind that Barth and Brunner have stimulated. Though any reader of these three men will discover many likenesses—they are all critical of fundamentalism, likewise of endeavors to create and to define religion by intellectual syncretisms—still it is the case that Bultmann accuses Barth of saving the gospel from "the acids of modernity" by doing violence to the meaning of the New Testament.[4] But more than this, Bultmann accuses his contemporaries of indirectly strengthening an old mythological system,

[2]*Christian Faith and Natural Science*, p. 24. The English translation (SCM Press) was published in London, 1953.

[3]Bultmann notes some of these efforts himself. Cf., *Kerygma and Myth, A Theological Debate*, edited by H. W. Bartsch, translated by R. H. Fuller (London, S.P.C.K.: 1953). The essay by Bultmann (pp. 1-44) is herein examined by five other students of theology.

[4]Using the title in *Kerygma and Myth*, I shall hereafter refer to Bultmann's essay as "NT and Mythology." Note the criticism of Barth, pp. 9-10, again p. 107.

that of the New Testament, which sooner or later is again going to be recognized for what it is.[5] Instead of a temporary
diversionary move—more festivities on the deck, more glorious
music—Bultmann insists upon an even more radical Biblical
study and criticism.

Biblical religion comes in Biblical language. Though Bultmann is the first to insist that the pastor must preach the
"kerygma" of the New Testament, still he does not advocate
the use of Biblical language in the pulpit. For the latter de-
ceives. Bultmann says: "If the truth of the New Testament
proclamation is to be preserved, the only way is to demythologize it."[6] Every successful sermon is in fact already a successful demythologization of the New Testament. If it is not, then
the sermon, in a degree at least, fails. To preach the Gospel is
not, therefore, to preach in New Testament language nor is it to
preach the Biblical message as it once was preached. To revive
a kind of Biblical language as Barth and others have done is
to indulge a cultic and dogmatic tradition which in its replete-
ness gives a first century mythology a twentieth-century expression.

Bultmann is a complex author and student. Being a highly
trained Biblical scholar and long known for his *form-Geschichte*
talents, he nonetheless carries on a double-barrelled polemic:
on the one side within the relatively narrow confines of technical Biblical scholarship and theology, and, on the other,
against any kind of obscurantism, theological or otherwise, which

---

[5]R. G. Smith, "What is Demythologizing?", *Theology Today*, X, No. 1, pp.
37-39.

[6]Bultmann, *Op. cit.* p. 10. It may be appropriate to note here that the word
"kerygma" means broadly "gospel' or "message." The question is whether
the gospel is a myth.

seems to confuse the preaching task.[7] His demythologizing essay is addressed to scholars in the interest of the homiletic task. Much of Biblical scholarship he finds not radical enough. His essay calls for the most exacting and honest kind of historical and textual research in order that the "kerygma" can be truly evangelical and persuasive. He wants to save the evangel from the fate deserving a mythology.

II

But now the question is—what is the preaching problem? Bultmann believes that there is a kerygma in the New Testament and that this is the reason for, and subject matter of, preaching. To this extent, he is a Biblical believer and theologian. He is not sympathetic with extrapolating—there must be exegesis of the New Testament or there is no Christianity at all. But the difficulties are numerous. For the rudiments of the life of Jesus in the Gospels, everything said about him by Paul and other epistle writers, is already an interpretative account. There is no simple story within a complexity, no non-interpretative historical and synoptic story to be contrasted with a Pauline or Johannine theological account. Bultmann long ago dispatched the thesis of so many of his generation, viz., that the New Testament's historical Jesus could be separated from the theological Christ, and this within the New Testament itself. But granted this, his demythologizing essay goes even further. It is not that historical fact and theological interpreta-

[7]Besides A. N. Hunter's survey of N.T. research in *Interpreting the New Testament* (SCM, 1951) there are also interesting summaries of Bultmann's importance to be found in several of the books of Vincent Taylor. Note his *The Formation of the Gospel Tradition*, esp. Chap. I, "A Survey of Recent Research." Compare F. C. Grant's *Form Criticism* (1934) where Grant also relates B. to other scholars. Other works of Taylor, e.g., his *The Gospels* (London, 1952, 7th ed.) pp. 7-22, and *The Names of Jesus* (London, 1953), *Jesus and His Sacrifice*, 2nd edition (London, 1951). Karl Barth has responded several times to Bultmann's criticisms, often with praise for his skill—cf. Henderson's *Myth in the New Testament*, p. 21; also in several recent essays scattered in European theological journals.

tion are inextricably tangled—rather it is that both of these are entangled in a language that is downright mythological. Granted that so-called liberal theologians were mistaken in believing that the historical Jesus, or sentences about Him, was or were the burden of synoptic literature, Bultmann finds likewise the view that the New Testament is a long confession, and as confession normative or determinative of subsequent readers' belief, also a mistake. To make its language normative for subsequent Christian's confessions is the mistake of modern Biblicism. Both positions disregard the fact that the story told in the New Testament is to any contemporary reader or listener (i.e., not only university professors and students) a tissue of mythology.

Naturally one must wonder what Bultmann means by mythology. He does not leave one in much doubt. The use of electric light and of the radio, of modern surgical and medical discoveries, is enough to give a clue. Their use makes simultaneous belief in the New Testament world of demons and spirits impossible.[8] Bultmann apparently means by "impossible" here, not logically contradictory or rationally inconceivable (though these may also be the case), but psychologically impossible. People cannot get themselves to believe in the mythological elements of the New Testament any longer; for there is nothing in the contemporary environment and culture which sustains their persuasiveness. It is not simply that scientific truth claims about the world are different than earlier truth claims—this effects only a minority of people—but also that the world about us, for educated and uneducated alike, is now plotted and controlled, measured and traveled upon, in such a

[8]"N.T. and Mythology," p. 5. Also, see his footnotes on the same page. Note also Austin Farrer's paper, "An English Appreciation," in *Kerygma and Myth*, pp. 212-223. Emil Brunner, though opposing Bultmann, says that it is true that: "We no longer live in a world in which the stars can fall from Heaven" (*Eternal Hope*, p. 119, London, 1954).

manner that earlier mythologies are simply irrelevant to the majority. The point is that even if we say we believe the New Testament mythology, we do not use nor sustain that mythology by further conduct, and not even, according to Bultmann, by living as Christians. In other words our conduct today is predicated upon a world which is not significantly described for us by the New Testament language.

According to Bultmann, therefore, the preacher's problem is plain enough. On the one side, there is a New Testament message, couched in a rich mythological language; on the other side, there are the hearers, twentieth century men, who cannot believe the mythology in any significant sense because it is neither true nor false, neither valid nor invalid. What is this mythology? Broadly, it is the New Testament's cosmology, the world conceived as a three-story structure, earth in the center, heaven above, hell below. But more than this, it is the panoply of views which construes the activities of earth as caused by supernatural forces and the activities of God and Satan. All kinds of things—Christ's birth of a Virgin, His power, the efficacy of His death, His resurrection, His exaltation at the right hand of God, death as a consequence of sin, Christ's pre-existence—all of these and more exemplify the language and thought of mythology.[9] The point is that preaching is for the purpose of communicating concerning the event of redemption. But if the mythological view of the world is obsolete, can this redemptive story be any longer told? And with or without the myth? If the myth is necessary men can neither accept the Gospel nor can they reject it. They instead will be and are scandalized by the myth, not the redemptive deeds. Bultmann believes therefore that the preacher's task is to demythologize

---

[9]*Op. cit.*, pp. 1-2. Also see the article by Dinkler for modifications. Note, too, Bultmann's remarks in the section called "Kerygma of the Hellenistic Church," *Theology of the N.T.*, vol. I, esp. pp. 121-133, 164-183.

the New Testament. This is the practical task of theology, which task is performed most significantly when it is done every Sunday in the pulpit. Bultmann is for a kind of "applied theology."

Bultmann's argument is, therefore, that we must demythologize the New Testament in order to save the New Testament's message. This is not an unbeliever's attack upon the New Testament but a believer's. Bultmann is not a liberal, at least he would never admit it; for liberals by his definition were those who tried to correct specific misconceptions according to ostensibly true or more probable conceptions of given events and relations. It is pertinent to point out that Bultmann believes that every preacher, at least since the Renaissance, has demythologized a little every time he has spoken. But no one has done it radically enough and with the conviction permitted by awareness of the "kerygma." Bultmann urges that all mythology be stripped away—or almost all—in order that the redemptive message be left. Previous endeavors were piecemeal, eliminating the demons first perhaps, then the "up-ness" of heaven when astronomy showed that there was no absolute up or down, then the literalness of hell's flames, then the locus of hell, then— and so on. The protest of Barth was to the effect that the "kerygma" had no longer been preached because one could never be certain that there was something left which was not eliminable at a future date. Bultmann argues that both this kind of elimination and the return to naive acceptance of the New Testament as the kerygma are mistaken.[10] Bultmann is afraid that the Gospel is unintelligible for some because the Gospels are so. The responsibility of a contemporary theologian-preacher is to demythologize in a new way. We, these late readers, must use any and all criticism to discover the New Testament mythology, all of it and the complicity of every

[10]*Op. cit.*, p. 12.

writer of the New Testament within it, and then use this criticism to interpret the mythology.[11] But Bultmann also insists that we can do this in confidence because we know what the Gospel is.

In justice to Bultmann it is important to say that he does not intend quite what his words read. It is not mythology which disguises religiousness and hence mythology which must be interpreted—it is, rather, that the use of New Testament mythology has to be understood. It is not mythology which can be explained but it is the use of it which can be explained. The mythology of the New Testament is not intrinsically Christian.[12] It is a prescientific cosmology, the view of the world which once seemed verifiable and true to most men who thought. But the Christians (and certain Jewish apocalyptic and Gnostic thinkers[13]) were not simply presenting "an objective picture of the world as it is" but were trying to communicate the understanding of the Christian's situation and role in the world in which he lived. Mythology's truth claim has disappeared for modern readers, but it existed for most of the New Testament writers. But the New Testament is not an essay on cosmology and therefore ought not to be read as such. The New Testament is a kind of soteriological anthropology. The mythology was used not to express the truth about the cosmos but to express some truths about men. Therefore the interpretation of myth which Bultmann proposes is anthropological (and existential), not cosmological.[14] Bultmann insists that what Christian Scripture says about men is true.

Amos Wilder believes that Bultmann is too much of a

---

[11]*Op. cit.*, p. 12. It is interesting to read Bultmann's interpretations in other contexts, e.g., *Theology of the New Testament*, vol. I, esp. pp. 106-108.

[12]*Ibid.*, p. 3. Compare "The Nature of Myth," pp. 10-11.

[13]*Ibid.*, p. 15 and Bultmann's *Gnosis* (Eng. translation of his article which appears in Kittel's *Theologisches Worterbuch* London, 1952). In "Manuals from Kittel" series, Vol. V. See pp. 41ff. Also note his *Theology*, "passim."

[14]*Ibid.*, p. 10.

literalist in these matters and that the genuinely poetical character of the New Testament is being disregarded.[15] Bultmann's view is apparently that much of the present indicative language in the New Testament is plainly not true and whether we call it poetry as Wilder does or mythology is irrelevant. In either case, it still is not true. What he calls the "rough edges" of its mythology are illustrations of the fact that all of it cannot be true for it makes the text outright contradictory. He finds the kenosis of the pre-existent Son (Phil. 2) incompatible with the miracle narratives as proofs of his Messianic claims; the Virgin birth is inconsistent with the assertion of pre-existence; sometimes we are told that human life is determined by cosmic forces, other times we are challenged to a decision. The Pauline indicative is inconsistent with the Pauline imperative.[16] Whether as poetry or as fact, its sentences cannot be believed to be descriptively true, not at least if such inconsistencies as those noted are already present. Even poetry and the parable are not ends in themselves when used in religious context. Bultmann is convinced that whether as poetry or as science, much of the present indicative language of the New Testament is simply meaningless. To make it meaningful one would have to do one of two things: (a) destroy the whole of science and the culture and civilization science continues to produce; or (b) discover again the anthropological meaning of redemption in and through Christ. To de-scientize, to become anti-intellectual to the extent necessary for the first is simply impossible, even for the preacher. To demythologize is to become intellectually

---

[15]Note in passing Wilder's criticism in the 2nd ed. of *Eschatology and Ethics in the Teaching of Jesus* (N.Y., 1950), esp. pp. 64ff. Also, the last pages of Wilder's review of the German volume, *J. Bib. Lit.* 69; 113-126.

[16]This is discussed in *Jesus and the Word* and very succinctly in the article already noted, pp. 11-12. Brunner says the mythological language of the N.T. is: "This massively tangible vividness of language" in order to make clear "the livingness of God." He also excuses the kind of inconsistencies B. refers to on this ground (Brunner, *Eternal Hope*, p. 116).

scrupulous. This is difficult but not impossible, even for the preacher and perhaps without the Holy Spirit. To discover the redemptive significance of Christ is to discover also the clue for the use of mythological language. But this does not justify using it ourselves. In fact, to know the meaning of redemption now is to know why one cannot use mythology any longer to convey it.

Bultmann believes that what he chooses to call "the understanding of man's place in the world" can now be stated more clearly than heretofore. What difference the Christ-event, His birth, life, death, made to the existence of men was once told cosmologically. The business of existing humanly without faith and with faith in Him are genuine and live alternatives. Both alternatives were once described within a three-story-world context, in which a Virgin was impregnated from above, the heavens shook in response to human malignancy, the Christ Himself was of cosmic dimension. Now the world is no longer felt nor conceived as such a place. It does not exist for one's daily emotions, one's daily thoughts, or one's actions. Bultmann does not think it should exist for one's Sunday emotions or thoughts either. Even if the physical world is now described and used within a more neutral set of categories, still there is the possibility of existing with faith and existing without it. Is it the case that having faith really means believing in a three-story universe? That Jesus went up? That there are spiritual bodies and realms of light? Bultmann thinks not and argues that preaching can properly dispense with mythology by always distinguishing between a human life without faith and one with it, both within the world as we understand it to be. Anyway, says Bultmann in effect, every preacher who ever makes sense to his congregation does this already. He is a de-mythologizer without knowing it![17]

III

What is life without faith? It is life in the "world," which is a "world" of corruption and sin. But for the Christian it is not as it was for the gnostics, "matter" which is the cause of sin. It is rather that the "world" is the name for all that surrounds a man which causes him "to live after the flesh."[18] Bultmann, following St. Paul, argues that such a life may be variegated—"there is the crude life of sensual pleasure and there is the refined way of basing one's life on the pride of achievement, on the 'works of the law' "—but the variety is unified by the fact that every such life is weighed down by anxiety.[19] The sinful life is an anxious life, in which all talents and opportunities are used to find security and confidence. All of this produces an incongruity because the actual human situation is that man is not secure at all. By not admitting and facing the facts of uncertainty and insecurity a man loses "his true life" and becomes the veritable slave of the very sphere he wished to master. "Worldliness" and the "world" acquire status and meaning in virtue of the investment of the enthusiasm of large numbers of people in principles, in constitutions, in points of view, in all kinds of absolutes and supposed invariants, in goodwill, fellowship, and other ameliorating virtues, which are believed to be secure if not certain, certain if not secure, sometimes both, in a world where men are not. "This is the way in which 'powers' which dominate human life come into being, and as such they acquire the character of mythical entities."[20] The sacredness of property, the view that rights are divine, that

---

[17]Note Bultmann's succinct replies to Schniewind, who had raised rather obvious critical points against him. Cf. op. cit., pp. 102-124.
[18]Romans 5-6 and Bultmann, Op. cit., pp. 17-19.
[19]I Cor. 7:32ff and Bultmann again, ibid.
[20]Op. cit., pp. 18-19.

virtue must win—these are contrivances to aid in the pursuit of security. The irony of history as Bultmann discerns it lies in the fact that wars and others forms of conflict between persons are an expression of our attempts "to secure visible security," which attempts are at another man's expense. Thus it is that even the other man's existence, in many circumstances, becomes a threat to my own. New Testament mythology is in part a consequence of the same sinfulness. Believers, too, create a "world" for themselves which has a different mien than the actual world has. Everyone is threatened by the actual state of affairs. New Testament literature reflects the "worldliness" of human subjects who are unable to live in the world as it really is.

Bultmann is not very optimistic about changing the structure of human societies or of human nature, nor of removing the actual limits of physical existence. He does not think that securities can be produced or that men can be so contrived that the insecurities will not appear as insecurities. Again it is quite clear that Bultmann does not hold to the view that knowledge removes insecurities. His view of science and its role in culture is to the effect that it does not remove "worldliness" but rather augments human talent and opportunities without really directing them. Likewise, learning does the same for the man of faith. Science and cognition do not directly produce worldliness nor do they destroy it. The point, therefore, in respect to the New Testament is that science destroys neither the opportunities for worldliness nor for faith, but only the cognitive claims for the prescientific cosmology.

As preachers and confessors of faithful living the New Testament authors told about the author and object of faith, Jesus Christ, in language which was persuasive and relevant, some of which language we now recognize as mythological.

What looked cognitively reliable was given a richer investment, a wider and deeper significance, than cognition itself could provide. The motives that made what was cognitively probable also seem religiously necessary were "worldly" motives, i.e., motives growing out of the sinful reluctance to see the actual world as insecure as it in fact is. Both worldliness and Christianity were once understood within a kind of mythology. But the Christian church has given this mythology status by commending uncritically the Bible. The question is whether we can now admit the incertitude and the insecurities. If so we ought to be able to demythologize the New Testament and also contemporary forms of worldliness.

The life of faith is life within the same incertitudes but without the anxieties. "Such a life," says Bultmann, "means the abandonment of all self-contrived security."[21] This is life in the Spirit, the life of faith. It means our future is not a threat, it becomes instead open and acceptable as a good gift. It means deliverance from the past (forgiveness) and from the pursuits of all the securities our talents and busyness can purchase. This is a kind of detachment, not asceticism, from the world, where all things become lawful but where nothing brings the self under its power.[22] The uncertainties remain uncertainties, the insecurities also endure, but the person is no longer anxious. The "world" becomes no longer important and determinative. In fact, Paul avers that it is crucified to him and he to it. This for Bultmann is "eschatological existence" and the meaning of being a new creature. Faith is the victory that overcomes the world.

[21]*Op. cit.*, p. 19. Note also Bultmann's essays on these same themes in *Essays, Philosophical and Theological*, translated by J. C. G. Greig (New York, MacMillan Co.: 1955).

[22]Bultmann cites *I Cor.*, chapters 7:29-31, 3:21-23, 6:12, etc. Note his remarks, pp. 19-22. For amplification note his little book on "gnosis" which contrasts the Christians and gnostics on these very points. Again, too, see his *Theology*, especially on the second century church.

The New Testament is somewhat cooperative with Bultmann on these points. He discerns a change from the synoptic gospels to John which frees progressively Jesus, the "last" judgment, the Kingdom of Heaven, from a cosmic process and claims that all of these are present realities, realizable in faithful existing. With Charles H. Dodd, Bultmann seems to be urging that John has discovered that there is "a realized eschatology," where everything outward remains as before, but where since the coming of Jesus, the world has no power over men. The fourth gospel is a kind of prolegomenon to demythologizing—it "carries this process to a logical conclusion by competely eliminating every trace of apocalyptic eschatology."[23] But its language is not completely indicative because the life of faith is not a possession, it is a process. It needs the imperative to complete it. It is a possibility to be appropriated by daily resolve—not any longer only a supernatural act to be brought about at the end of a cosmic process. The Christian soteriology even in the New Testament, if Bultmann's description is correct, is to be encountered not passively, but actively, not when men are spectators to it but when they are participators with Him by their own existing. Paul is crucified with Christ—and so are we. But without Christ, we are not crucified to the world at all; instead, we are in bondage to the world and all that it is. Faith, by detaching man from "worldliness," makes him capable of fellowship. Delivered from anxiety and the necessity of securing himself, he also becomes free to love and to enjoy others. Hence, faith is "working through love" and this too means being a "new creature."[24] The same faith which frees a man from worldliness and anxiety ought to emancipate him from the mythology of the New Testament, which at best was only a poor device to secure the "kerygma" concerning Jesus.

[23]*Op. cit.*, p. 20.
[24]*Ibid.*, p. 22.

IV

Bultmann believes that the New Testament even when translated into modern idiom tells the story of redemption as though it were primarily an event in the cosmos. His critics notwithstanding, Bultmann is not a "gnostic," who is saying that Christianity is only an event within the reflection of men. Christ was a real historical man. He lived, He died, and it is reputed that He moved again among men. But despite the historicity of Jesus, Bultmann finds the cosmological additions at least, gratuitous, and at most, downright deceptive. He wishes, therefore, to interpret every redemptive phase of the historical Christ's life and existence, every aspect of the New Testament authors' faith in His redemptive activity, in language which makes it clear that these are "real experiences in human life."[25] The experiences in human life are remarkably the same throughout the generations because the world is as uncertain as ever it was.

Preaching is apparently the art of telling the story of Jesus and the redemptive life engendered by Him in language which will be anthropological rather than cosmological. Theological assertions are, to put it in another way, actually assertions about human life.[26] In characteristically sharp and provocative manner, Bultmann insists that his endeavor to demythologize is "a perfect parallel" to St. Paul's and Luther's doctrine of justification by faith alone. Without denying the objective and historical existence of Jesus, without denying that there is salvation only in Christ, Bultmann still insists that these two assertions do not implicate one in the prescientific cosmology of the New Testament. The proof value of that cosmology is now gone. Bultmann avers to having carried the doctrine of justification

[25]Again in Bultmann's reply, p. 106. Note the original essay, pp. 23-33.
[26]Here Bultmann uses an accusation of Barth to make clear his own point, p. 110.

by faith to "its logical conclusion in the field of epistemology."[27]
Neither works nor cosmic acts nor a conspiracy of both justify
either one's life or one's thoughts. God comes to men in the
Word, which for us includes the New Testament words about
Jesus, the historical man. But the ground of faith and the object of faith are the same—even though they do not appear
so to the New Testament writers—at least as their text reads.
For them the object of the faith was the same Jesus but they
provided another ground (or one might say, a set of reasons),
a trans-historical process in which both that object and they,
were engaged. This was their means of communicating the
story of Jesus. Their cosmology has now become a myth.[28]
They used it as proof for Jesus' nature and power and history
and always with the intention of showing that the affirmative
response of men to Him was deserved and praiseworthy.

Bultmann seems to be saying that this was bad religion because it did not trust the efficacy of Jesus or even His effective-
ness in the lives of men. Even the Apostles had to help Him
out a bit. Did they deceive? Did they lie? Not necessarily.
Bultmann only argues that theirs is the fault that redeemed
men also commit. They did not quite believe in God and sought
to justify themselves, if not by works, at least by ascertain-
able knowledge. Bultmann says: "The man who wishes to believe in God as his God must realize that he has nothing in his
hand on which to base his faith."[29] He cannot demand a proof.
All of this made for very bad epistemology, for it argued that
God was a cognitive object, that certain cosmological events
and processes were holy. Just as Luther taught that there are

[27]*Op. cit.,* p. 210-211.
[28]Note A. M. Hunter, *Interpreting the New Testament,* 1900-1950 (London
    1951) for discussion about the dissatisfaction of Biblical scholars with a
    "theology-less" New Testament text, esp. pp. 124-140. For independent judg-
    ment, see, too, Hoskyns and Davies, *Riddle of the New Testament,* new ed.,
    1949.
[29]Bultmann, op. cit., p. 21.

no holy places in the world so too have the epistemologists discovered the neutrality of place and event. But this is to those who have no faith. With faith the earth is the Lord's, and nature and history are, contrary to appearance, the field of divine activity. But it is not the world which changes because of Christ but rather the men within it who are changed.

The invisibility of God ought rightly to exclude every myth which tries to make Him and His acts visible. God can only be believed upon in defiance of the appearances, just as justification of a sinner can only be believed upon in defiance of the accusations of the conscience. The only way to tell the story of Christ is to relate Him to men in such a way that to speak of God means simultaneously to speak of the existence of men.[30] Existence without Jesus is different from existence with Him—but to say as much is too abstract as it stands and seems to elicit a cosmology if abstractness is to be avoided. Rather we must say that the existence of a man, a man's life, is different without Jesus from what it is with Him. Here no cosmology needs to be added. All that is supposed is an anology "between the activity of God and that of man and between the fellowship of God and man and that of man with man."[31]

Bultmann wishes to make the preaching of a Christocentric and theological religion possible—logically and psychologically. The only way to do it is to forsake the mythology and stick to the fact that Jesus is God because He makes and saves a man's existence. To put it the other way around, namely, that He makes and saves a man's existence because He is God, born of a Virgin, a star marked His birth, He possessed miraculous powers, He descended and ascended—this is to ask men to lose their intelligences in order to save their lives. Furthermore, it

---

[30]Op. cit., p. 210. Also, pp. 196 ff. re "Language . . ."

[31]Op. cit., p. 197. Bultmann notes Frank's *Philosophical Understanding and Religious Truth* (Oxford University Press, 1945) as corroboration.

is to be scandalized on the wrong points. And, besides, this is not the foolishness which bothered the Greeks. To live by dying to the world is foolishness enough. By preaching Jesus Christ one again makes good the tidings; for the promise is that we can lose our anxiety and dread of living in an insecure world and instead enjoy the same world in faith because of Jesus Christ.

V

Perhaps a brief summary of Bultmann's argument is now in order. He argues on the basis of the accumulated historical, linguistic, and theological studies of Biblical literature that there is a message to be believed. His point is made with a confidence born of a half century of preoccupation with these issues himself. It means, among other things, that the analysis of the texts in a critical spirit has not destroyed the object of faith as so many conservative and earnest people have frequently said. Instead there is something corresponding to human faith— there is a message within the Scripture and it remains after the critical studies have been performed.

By itself, this contention of Bultmann is important. It speaks the mind of the majority of Bible students of our day and countermands the views that has had an undeserved popularity among sophisticated people, namely, that analytic studies would completely annihilate the faith of the Christian Church. Rowley's insistence that there is a unity to Biblical literature, though argued on different grounds, parallels Bultmann's argument, and more studies to the same effect could be cited. The meaning of such a shift in emphasis in the sciences concerning religion is difficult to assess, but, by itself, it has the effect of strengthening the nobility of intellectual effort against all of those who conclude too quickly that faith survives only in blindness and ignorance.

Furthermore, Bultmann has cogently argued that the matrix in which the message of salvation comes is full of the signs of humanity, so full in fact that the Bible itself is even mythological. This latter point is not an easy one to accept nor to reject. Most of Bultmann's readers find themselves frankly puzzled by this turn in the argument. Anyone concerned about this would do well to consult the six volumes containing the disputations of Bultmann's colleagues and critics on the issue.[32] Before concluding lightly that Bultmann is right other people ought to be consulted.

One consideration apparently overlooked by Bultmann altogether is the fact that all of us have continually to speak about the world in at least two different ways. On the one side, we consider the world in the light of our daily interests and the common sense by which we have to make necessary decisions. On the other side, we consider the world detachedly and disinterestedly and without allowing common sense to enter in at all. The first kind of language is anthropomorphic and interestful; the other is abstract and objective. Bultmann seems to be saying that the language of the Bible is not the language of science. Here we can all agree and without suffering any loss whatsoever. But to move to the next point of saying that it is mythological goes way too far. For it is not really necessary nor illuminating to say this. The Bible tells us what the world is to those who believe in God. The Bible contains the language of faithful people who dare to think that all things, natural and supernatural, work together for good to those who love God.

This side of the question has not been adequately explored by Bultmann. He leaves one with the gnawing doubt that de-

[32]*Kerygma und Mythos*, 1948 through 1955. These are published by Herbert Reich, Hamburg, Germany.

spite the grandeur of his conception there is something wanting respecting his understanding of exactly what theology is. For Bultmann is surely one of the most exciting scholars in our day; but part of the excitement is caused by a confusion which he continues, one which is part of the history of German religious scholarship and culture. Bultmann does not finally distinguish sharply enough between reflection and language about the Bible (and what it says) and the message of the Bible, which is the language of faith. His distinction between kerygma and mythology is again interesting; but it will not bear scrutiny, unless it can be shown specifically that mythology is actually about the kerygma and not the kerygma itself. But theology is not necessarily about the kerygma. Theology and preaching are continuous; and both, in turn, are distinguishible from scholarship about preaching and theology. If the Bible contains bad language about religious matters, then it may well be mythological; and if this is Bultmann's claim, then his view of mythology is the conventional one.

The fact remains that Bultmann has vivified contemporary theological discussion in Europe. It is to be hoped that more attention will be given to the matter of exactly what theology and preaching are; and if Bultmann will force discussion upon such issues, then even his errors might be useful. But on some other specific points, he has already proved a boon. For example, he has argued that scholarship, Biblical and historical, does not produce the kerygmatic stuff. Despite his radicalness, Bultmann still argues the Christian's dependence upon the Scripture. Also, Bultmann's words about mythology are in the nature of a solemn warning to the learned Christians, and not least the professional theologians. For the learned men want safeguards for everything, including their faith. Bultmann believes that the New Testament writers, like most churchmen since, were really

faithless and that, in the absence of vivid faith, they were trying
to erect cognitive surrogates. Perchance Bultmann's words will
be a warning to theologians, among others, who believe more
in intellectual formulations than they do in God.

But, there is more: Bultmann has unified historical and
Biblical studies, philosophical research, and a variety of theological inquiries. He has done this in at least two ways. First,
he has done all of them himself; second, he has proposed what
turn out to be some common problems. Rightly or wrongly, he
has attacked the separateness of religious disciplines by new
efforts and new definitions of subject matter and issues.

Bultmann has helped his readers to see that the New Testament is a homiletical treatise, confessional, non-scientific in intent, persuasive rather than hypothetical. Simultaneously and
paradoxically, he has tried to persuade preachers from using the
New Testament homiletically, for then, according to his argument, the mythology will obtrude and the kerygma will be
lost. What he should be saying instead is that even the passion
of the Apostles will not suffice for the readers. Whether this
requires the warnings about mythology is another matter altogether.

Lastly, Bultmann has made courage a virtue again, for
clergy and for professors. He has dared the radical explanation
and brought vivacity into theological dispute. Not least of his
success, as it is presently counted, lies in the novelty of his
thought and the pungency of his expression. Nonetheless, he
has also sought to help the preacher. Rather than giving words
to him, he has proposed their scrutiny. In a good sense, he has
made preaching harder. Even his suggestion that preaching demands not more second-hand talk, that which he calls mythology, but anthropology, i.e., words about oneself who is a faithful
believer in the Lord Jesus, are straightening. The necessary con-

dition for preaching is that one have faith himself. With all of his learning, Bultmann manages enough grace to make us aware that learning is no substitute for a personal quality. And if a technical theologian can do this, then we are in his debt. It seems odd to be told what we always know, were it not for the fact that our forgetfulness is so constant too. If one is going to be Christian, one must, at the very least, be religious. Theology is not a substitute for faith; but Bultmann need not have called it mythology to make that point.

CHAPTER FOURTEEN

Personality and Faith Kierkegaard

Kierkegaard is one of those rare men of reflection—he is too many-sided ever to be a founder of a school of thought. He is not quite properly Lutheran, certainly not scholastic enough; nor is he only an existentialist or even pre-Barthian or anti-metaphysical or an irrationalist. He illustrates the motto which prefaces *The Philosophical Fragments*, "Better well hung than ill wed." Though many of his readers have tried to assimilate him to commodious categories, he does not quite fit. For surely no author with such a regard for logicality can be justly described simply as an irrationalist; neither can a devotee of intellectual tradition and a person of catholic tastes and sympathies be seen adequately only as a man of revolt, existentialist or otherwise; and though there is an "either/or" bringing distinctiveness to human discourse and choice, yet it must be remembered that Kierkegaard believed in the powers of personality to synthesize otherwise discrepant factors. Though tragedy and suffering were not alien to him, still he was convinced that Christianity was a happiness view and that faith is the victory which overcomes the world.

To describe Kierkegaard's significance for theology has been made difficult rather than easy by the scholarship about him. For often he has been claimed to be Lutheran or on the road to Rome, anti-intellectual or too intellectual, anti-church or pro-Augustine, too psychological or too theological or even both. Actually Kierkegaard is much better as a theologian than his theological critics and adherents make him out to be. He is a radical thinker. He is more concerned with the sub-structures than with the super-structures and, on almost every page, his interest is directed toward that kind of issue which is elemental and from which perhaps several intellectual elaborations can be made. Simply because he talks about matters common to so many positions taken by schoolish thinkers, it becomes almost an adventure to find him a therapeutic but Christian positivist, or a neo-orthodox theologian, or the father of existentialism. Besides being mistaken most of such claims are trivial and an indictment of the scholar who makes them.

A most general point about Kierkegaard perhaps deserves to be remembered. Kierkegaard was, intellectually considered, a diacritical thinker. He was able to make and to sustain distinctions. He excelled in the use of diagnostic abilities and was able throughout his career (brief as it was—he began writing in 1841-42 and was done about nine years later) to ferret out the skein of possibilities with the utmost of logical rigor. This is the aristocratic and technical side of the man and his authorship. Here he sought to be rigorous, exacting, precise, in fact everything that any scrupulous man of intelligence discovers necessary for intellectual transparency. But the other side, and equally important, was his abiding interest in the synthesis proposed by Christianity for human personality. At once Kierkegaard commanded those dialectic and pathetic (i.e., capacities for pathos) talents which enabled him to indulge and yet to study those pervading emotions and commandeering interests which make existing distinctively human. The point then is that Kierkegaard combined an analytic intelligence with an ethico-religious and synthesizing passion. His authorship endeavors to dignify as well as to express the nobility of the simultaneity of factors within the personality, and especially as this is constituted by faith in Jesus Christ.

All of this should caution the reader against too quickly summarizing Kierkegaard's thought. Reflection moves by distinctions and exclusions and bifurcations but existence is, like the mock turtle soup of which one of his pseudonyms speaks, full of everything. Knowing that the exclusions in thought might not entail exclusions in being, Kierkegaard is very wary indeed in circumscribing what is real. Thus he does not deny metaphysics all meaning simply because he denies that thought and reality are one. Nor does he deny the objectivity of Jesus, of actual existence, of canons of thought, simply because he notes the importance of subjectivity and the difficulties of the ontological logic of his day. And he is not quite a sectarian and a voluntarist on distinctively Christian matters simply because he notes intellectual and ethical discrepancies on matters like the Church and the sacraments. But, neither is he meekly traditional here either.

Surely Kierkegaard was a wise man. He knew that intellectual extremes were daring and even exciting but here common sense was his guide. His intellectual affirmations were tentative and subject to recall. But ethically and religiously he sought decisiveness and maximal risk-taking. The leap of faith was an act whereby the personality constituted itself, whereby character was formed. To keep oneself ethically decisive while admitting intellectual uncertainty was part of Kierkegaard's admonition towards the good life. The fact that an erstwhile

Christian culture had blurred this difference and the fact that philosophers had proposed ontological understanding, the understanding of being itself, as the bridging of the gap, led Kierkegaard to his task of reintroducing Christianity into Christendom and making numerous viable intellectual distinctions all over again.

Four issues will be here adumbrated. Though these might indicate Kierkegaard's relevance to contemporary theology, still more it is hoped that they may incite that kind of enthusiastic attention deserving a man of pervading Christian compassion who was simultaneously an aristocrat among the "cognoscendi."

I

First it ought to be noted that Kierkegaard addressed himself to the problem of the meaning of religious discourse. It is a commonplace among students of eighteenth and nineteenth century theological literature to note the difference between saving theology by converting its statements into metaphysical claims on the one hand and historical claims on the other. The Gnostics had even tried, much earlier, to vindicate theological claims by showing that no historical claims were essential. And today, once again, there are fervent endeavors among the theologically inclined to show that theology can be demythologized and, further, that commitment to Jesus Christ does not entail a commitment to a metaphysical schematism. All of this is part of the large and vexing inquiry into the meaning of religious discourse.

It is perhaps a dubious distinction to impose upon an author, namely, that he wrote on a topic relevant to men of a century later. Besides, Kierkegaard wrote on this topic only indirectly and in consequence of a concern with the question of the locus of religiousness. Though Kierkegaard knew too that the Christian religion had permeated our customs, our literature, and our language with glory and hope, he was not content to let the contemplation of these objectivities be the primary religious act. He contended against Hegel, not so much because his empirical descriptions were either wrong or absurd, but, rather, because Hegel denied in his grandiose interpretation the religiousness of human subjectivity. It is Kierkegaard's merit to have stressed the fact that theological language, whether this be the language of the Bible or the more formal discourse of the theologian, corresponds also to human subjectivity.

Unlike other thinkers who make a point by excluding too much, Kierkegaard does not deny the possibility of objective reference to theological language. However, his point is a pregnant one, and fraught with all kinds of as yet unexplored implications, namely, that religious discourse is not religious because it conveys results. The point of religious language is not to communicate results as much as it is to stimulate the process of experience and thought which will reconstitute human personality. Ethico-religious truth is, in other words, not a quality of the language itself but is rather the process, the striving of the human subject to be a definitive individual.

Though this kind of point is frequently made, and usually clumsily, it is to Kierkegaard's credit that he makes it with both an aristocratic intellectual intent of clarifying the muddle that the learned create on these matters, and an earnest religious endeavor of showing that the simple man as well as the learned share the condition in their subjectivity for the realization of the highest truth which Jesus Christ is. Kierkegaard had no sympathy with Spinoza's religion in which God is actually the sum total of the logical predicates available to an aristocratic mind. Likewise, the translation of the language of Christianity into that of the logic of historical existence, which Hegel tried to effect, Kierkegaard protests on both intellectual and moral grounds.

But, as yet, Kierkegaard is relatively untried on these matters. However, one hundred years ago he admitted the objective uncertainty of theological pronouncements and hence was not disturbed by Biblical criticism of his day nor would he be chagrined by the confessions of intellectual incertitude in ours; but, withal, he noted that the primary question was the quality of one's own life, his own subjectivity, and that no theological sentence was religious in meaning until the appropriation process was stimulated and human passion aroused.

I am bold enough to suggest that recent theology is positively amateurish on these matters. Kierkegaard's epistemological and technical acumen holds a great promise for future formal inquiries upon which so much theology depends. But even more than this, Kierkegaard was a master at etching out the devotional requisites of Christian religiousness and not least of his disinterestedness is expended on the task of reflecting himself out of the esthetic, the philosophic, and the aristocratic, and back again into the devotional and the simple.

II

A second consideration marking Kierkegaard's theological relevance is his disclosure of the importance of passions and interests. Few authors have been so marvelously equipped for this kind of task as that Dane. He wrote effortlessly and gives the impression of writing with the immediacy that the bird sings and the flower spreads its fragrance. It is no wonder that he thought of himself as a poet. Once his literary goal became clear, his authorship comes forth almost completely free of those niggardly and finite calculations marring so many artistic and literary productivities. He wrote out of his own inwardness which was rich indeed and in a style not calculated to please his public but one adequate to his own insight. But, for this very reason, he succeeds in writing out of his own pathos and writing his way into the pathos of another individual, his reader. If nothing else, the Kierkegaardian literature is so rich in pathos, so replete with those dimensions of human subjectivity that are truly universal, so expressive of refined passions and concerns, that here alone it will bridge long spans of time and continue to challenge moral turpitude and laxity.

Such honesty, sincerity, and flaming concern, expended as it is in an authorship which defines religious truth not as sentences to be learned but as dynamic becoming of the self, are theologically important by themselves. But Kierkegaard did more. He described the causal and efficacious role of interests and passions in the greatest detail. He brings together what are otherwise so often separated in Christian tradition. For him, the emphasis upon the objectivity of Jesus' existence, of the Atonement, and other divine acts, does not deny the existence nor the significance of subjectivity. In fact, it is his intent not to correct Protestant theology here as much as it is to supplement its account by showing that subjectivity too can be orderly, that it can and indeed, must, predispose the person. Instead of distrusting subjectivity as Lutheran dogmatics and Church practice suggest, Kierkegaard delineates carefully the role of despair, of dread, of guilt, this to make clear that no one is a sinner deductively and only because the dogma says that all men are sinners. A subjective state does correspond and Kierkegaard is apt at pointing it out, all the while skillfully noting the differences as various objectivities, laws, mores, God, Christ, are engaged.

But more than this, Kierkegaard notes too that the content of Christian religiousness is finally passional and interestful, not conceptual. Not only are modes of subjectivity the cause of religious striving but the appropriation of religious teaching, and of anything else religious which is objective and social, leads to another mode of subjectivity. Even love, the *agape* of the New Testament, must be a passion. Kierkegaard felt a responsibility as author to lead his reader out of subjectivity and into the contemplation of objectivities only for the sake of the new subjectivity which Christian faith, hope, and love are. Surely this is a distinctive note in theological and philosophical writing and worthy of very careful attention. Few authors have been as successful in saying this in a congruent manner as was Kierkegaard. For he destroys as he moves along his own authority and calculates the effect of his writing in such a way as to augment the passional response within the reader.

Kierkegaard, as also noted in the previous section, is here proposing a new basis for the discussion of theological issues. In centuries past, when theologians were able to talk with impunity about the final and efficient causes of nature (this because the physicists already did so), when man of religious learning could espouse easily the fortunes of God in the progress of men, then there seemed little reason to believe that human subjectivity was naught else than a mirror, confused and distorting indeed, of the passing scene. But Kierkegaard is suggesting that the inner life is not a mirror of the outer existence. It is not a chaos, not a random or caused array. Kierkegaard's literature is the disclosure of the life of subjectivity as a cosmos, capable of being mapped and described, in some respects independent and in ethico-religious senses most important of all. By saying that an interest in and a passion for existing is the reality that men can actually practice and own, Kierkegaard proposes a kind of metaphysics, not only compatible with

Christianity and the New Testament, but also a new point of departure for theological discussion.

III

It may seem amiss to say it but Kierkegaard seems also to have rediscovered the pragmatic significance of the person of Jesus Christ. All kinds of books can be written about Jesus Christ just as they can about Plato, each book taking account of the history of the teachings, of institutions, of the criticisms of either, and all of this being a documentation of the significance of the man. Each book thus written is in turn an item in history to be understood again as a part of the growing significance of the man. But it is Kierkegaard's point that as true as the respective historical accounts of Plato's and Christ's significances might be, still this is not the proper way to describe the bearing upon human interests of the person of Jesus Christ. As important as scholarship might be, Kierkegaard brings a correction to the view that grows up where religious studies are pursued and taught, namely, that by increasing the scope and broadening the grasp, the personal and intense religious response will follow as a matter of course.

Certainly it is true that Christianity has its own tradition and that this is both extensive and refined; likewise there is an institutionalizing of the idea which has resulted in the Church becoming a formidable power in the affairs of men; and not least, rightly or wrongly, there are external authorities, men and books, which are reputed to keep the keys to the treasures of life eternal. Kierkegaard neither denies nor affirms with enthusiasm the above views. But what he is concerned to point out is the fact that no one of these is, nor all of them together are, in such connection with the individual that the Christian's response is ever passionless, habitual, or trivial. Instead there is the person of Christ and He is the paradox. This latter word, "paradox," is intended by Kierkegaard to safeguard the uniqueness of the Christian's object of interest. Paradoxicality describes that kind of relation and object which Christianity and Christ are.

On the object side, Christ is the paradox because no premises offered to reflection can make loyalty and faith to Him a necessary and inevitable consequent. He is neither obviously God, nor inductively speaking, even the greatest man who ever lived. Even if He were the latter, still an absolute commitment would be incommensurate with the approximative and necessarily hypothetical conclusion. But on the subject's side, there is paradoxicality because He is the object of interest, offense or faith, scorn or worship, without that kind of justification which decisiveness seems to ask. The interest which He asks in His own existence and person, is an interest not congruent with self-interest nor is it congruent with that reason which we all invoke quite concretely as the reflectively organized common sense of mankind. The contrariety of interests on the subject's side is many-sided of course. Disinterested analysis and reflection suggest a suspension of decision while the guilt and concern going with it counsel the need for a resolute decision; it does not quite seem to be in one's own interest to deny oneself and his interests in order to save oneself. Jesus Christ seems to be asking that men live by dying, that they win by losing, that they get by giving.

Kierkegaard's theological fecundity is again rich on two sides. On the abstract and formal side, he has produced and argued with exactitude the doctrine of paradoxicality and several related doctrines which constitute in part, surely, the prolegomenon to future Christological discussion—even if like other prolegomena this one too may help to circumscribe the inventiveness and exuberance of speculative thinkers. But, on the ethical and practical side, Kierkegaard is even richer. There is an almost lavish outpouring of literature from his pen on the consequence in human existing of an active relation to and interest in the existence of Jesus Christ. This again does not lack exactness and form, but rather vindicates the view that Christian subjectivity has its esthetic features, its suppleness, its variants, and even its sophistication. Where most authors are pedestrian and flat-footed and at best can repeat Biblical rubrics with only slight elaboration, Kierkegaard can both illustrate in his own person and sketch for his reader the dramaturgical features of Christian inwardness.

Not least of the relevance of the figure of Jesus to the person is the fact that a response to Him is not exclusively intellectual, or emotional, or dutiful. It is to Kierkegaard's credit again to have corrected the intellectualism of Protestantism and brought ethicality and empirical behavior back into consideration. Kierkegaard insists that religiosity too is a living synthesis of the personality in thinking, feeling, and willing. The esthetic factors are not extirpated, the ethical is not abnegated; instead Kierkegaard delineates the richness of the faith relation by showing that even many sets of categories cannot quite exhaust it. All of this is testimony to the personality values which Kierkegaard discovers to be consequent to the contemporaneity with Jesus Christ.

The thesis that contemporaneity with Jesus is actually possible involves Kierkegaard as it has everyone who thinks about it in numerous problems, epistemological and theological. Kierkegaard repudiates the use, though not necessarily the truth, of the substance doctrines and other gambits of the past. Instead he suggests that Jesus Christ exists as the contemporary only when one's own interest and passion is Christ-like. His suggestion is that the historical Jesus when viewed detachedly and disinterestly is not the eternal contemporary. But when one forgives trespasses, as the prayer of our Lord suggests, then we are forgiven; when one loves an enemy, one is loved. But one is not loved because of one's own love, one is loved contemporaneously. Kierkegaard too is concerned to say that one's deeds do not merit God's attention. The presence of Christ is not a disinterestedly guaranteed and objectively warranted phenomenon. Again I can only urge that Kierkegaard's reflections here are most suggestive and seem to bear out the New Testament as well as augur well for further consideration.

IV

Last, and briefly, Kierkegaard has read exceedingly well the features of human existence. Many of the listeners in the pew have noted that things in the world are not quite the way the preacher has described them. When one hears the pulpit fulminating about the horrors of sin, and these horrors get no amplification other than that provided by either gross sensuality or misuse of public trust, then it certainly becomes difficult to fit the theological categories to every man. Kierkegaard corrected the interpretations, not by reforming the dogmas but by examining again the way it is we actually behave. Thus he sees us as sinners when we are sensual but also when we are most spiritual and moral. Nowhere does he suggest that sensuous delight in the things of the world is *ipso facto* sinful.

But all of this is part of his long essay in re-reading the human situation. Every issue he touches, the faith and reason controversy, the question of original sin, the significance of music, gets a new and creative treatment. If one analyzes all of this, it is surely the case that Kierkegaard makes his reader see that one's own personality, not history and not nature, is the locus for the presence of God. The larger orders may have their teleologies, God is undoubtedly present in all things occasioning their working together for good, but it is still men who must love God. Again, Kierkegaard does not deny in order to affirm —his domain is personality and he dares to believe that Christ died for every man and that the paramount concern must be to become a Christian. Once the inner teleology is taken care of, then the natural and historical scene may be read for what it is worth.

Hence it is that Christian faith is not alien to personality as Kierkegaard understands it. The otherness of God, the distinction between God and man, are not treated in anything but human terms. This must be remembered about Kierkegaard, for he is only mistakenly associated with these traditions which emphasize God's transcendance in non-human categories.

Perhaps few writers have said so much about the glory of our common humanity as Kierkegaard did. Not a little of that glory is evident in the very fact that so much can be known and said about being human and being Christian. For Kierkegaard too, being Christian was a human perfection, not to be gainsaid because it is human nor slighted because it is finally a matter of grace.

In a day when human nature is in such bad repute, when the very fountainhead of sin-talk seems to be Kierkegaard, it might be well to discover how careful he was, how anxious to do justice to the sensory capacities, the aesthetic refinement, the genial admixture of pluses and minuses that we all are. The diatribes in his literature are reserved for those who have levelled all the valleys, who have straightened all the paths, who have taken the heights and depths of personal expression away from their fellows. All of those who, impressed by the engines of society and anxious to secure conformity to God, country and duty, and who have slandered man by taking the adventure away—these are Kierkegaard's foes. That they include the clerics too, he was quick to note. His enthusiasms were, instead, for the restoration of passion, of expressiveness, of the individual's caring mightily. His literature is an attempt to restore the individual and his idiosyncracies to a place of honor. For it is by rubbing that Aladdin's lamp, one's own personality and subjectivity, that one discovers God in Christ reconciling the world and oneself unto Himself.

CHAPTER FIFTEEN

Philosophy and Faith: Schweitzer

Few men need so little said on their behalf as Albert Schweitzer. His life has such dramatic proportions that it seems almost Olympian and the work of a host of generous muses. While he is hailed as a kind of non-sectarian saint and praised for the successful use of many natural talents, it is almost forgotten that he is one of the most novel and original scholars of our day and that his scholarly productivity is both penetrating and massive, more than enough to secure for him an honored place in the annals of learning.

Strangely perhaps, the admiration so many persons feel for his resolute life of service has created a reluctance to examine in detail the validity of many of his intellectual offerings. Despite his work on Bach, his collaboration with Charles Widor on a widely-extolled annotated edition of Bach's organ works, his organ playing, his study of civilizations, still his most crucial work, that which makes one privy to those springs of character making him a force in the world—this lies within his philosophic and religious scholarship. This is relatively unknown by the many people who acclaim him.

Schweitzer long ago enunciated the necessary conditions for reflection on fundamental questions when he concluded as follows: "For nowhere save in the German temperament can there be found in the same perfection the living complex of conditions and factors—of philosophic thought, critical acumen, historical insight, and religious feeling—without which no deep theology is possible."[1] In singular fashion, Schweitzer illustrates this kind of German temperament most markedly. The combination of personality factors which are his makes him almost the realization of the eighteenth century universal man, one whose talents and interests are multiple and magnanimous.

Besides his natural talents, one must also reckon with his view of his own vocation. Finding the world "inexplicably mysterious and full of suffering," in both Europe and Africa, he goes on to say that his sadness is to have been born into a period of marked spiritual decadence. His conclusion from these two perceptions, which, he says, have cast shadows over his existence, is simple and clear: "I therefore stand and work in the world as one who aims at making men less shallow and morally better by making them think."[2] Throughout his busy lifetime, Schweitzer has expressed almost complete disagreement with everything exemplifying disdain for thinking and the intellectual life. Instead of conceiving the powers of the world to reside in numbers, unity, and greater exclusiveness, Schweitzer has argued that ideas have a spiritual worth and power, by which men may assuredly look a little inconvenient and uncanny, but also by which they become independent and noble. Schweitzer's religion is a synthesis of reflection and passion—he confesses to being a rationalist whose confidence in

[1]*The Quest of the Historical Jesus*, translated by W. Montgomery (London: 1910), p. 1.
[2]*Out of My Life and Thought*, translated by C. T. Campion (New York, 1933), p. 254.

thought is not destroyed but is strengthened by his Christian faith. With such a view, he seems to give a kind of justification for his own life and career too. For, in a very original way, his life is a synthesis of most radical scholarship and dramatic service to African natives.

II

Schweitzer exhibits to an outstanding degree the resolute patience, the dispassionateness, and the indefatigableness essential to scholarship. In addition, he has a many-sidedness and intensity — esthetically, intellectually, and ethically, which mark him off from the majority of men. It is typical of Schweitzer to decide at the age of twenty-one that his next nine years would be dedicated to pastoral work, science, and music. Thereafter he said: "I would dedicate the rest of my life to the service of my fellow men."

Unlike most people, he carried out this plan with determination. His decisions were sudden, in childhood and in maturity, but resolute. In order to complete his plan, he sat up many a night and kept himself awake with cold footbaths and strong coffee. One suspects that he had talent in addition.

Schweitzer was born in 1875; he made his resolution in 1896; therefore he had only through 1905 to get almost a life's work done. But he did it. In 1899 he wrote an important study of Kant's philosophy of religion; in 1901 a couple of short books on the relations between the Lord's Supper and beliefs about the end of time; in 1905 came the remarkable Bach study and in 1906 *The Quest of the Historical Jesus.* All of these approximate 2000 pages of seminal scholarship.

In later years, while a medical student and missionary doctor, Schweitzer added two long studies of the Apostle Paul, a two-volume treatise called *Civilization and Ethics,* several essays on Goethe, the book on Indian philosophy, plus augmented versions of "The Quest" and an enlarged German edition of his Bach volume (the first was written in French).

His autobiography, *Aus Meinem Leben und Denken,* and several reportorial books about his Africa sojourns are among the finest pieces of clear and beautiful German prose.[3] All in all, Schweitzer has written more than most major figures in the history of recent scholarship and this in addition to being an organ performer, a pastor, a teacher, an editor, a doctor, and a builder in the African wilds.

A little admiration for Schweitzer's accompuishments can be excused in almost any man; besides, he has done much of his work against great odds. Many times in the early days of his career he was without funds and physical help. But again remarkable doggedness and persistence seemed to carry him through.

But this is not to say that Schweitzer is always correct. Far be it from me to suggest this. All I propose here are a few elemental points which disclose, I believe, the proportions of his scholarship. These points seem to me to be distinct and might serve, therefore, as an egress into his authorship. These also give a clue to his motivations as a man. Whether he is right or not is another and complex matter.

Schweitzer is also an inordinately complex man religiously. Though there is something resembling a cultic adoration of him, still a few disclaimers ought to be filed. Popular views are to the effect that he has given up everything in order to be

---

[3]There are several of these pieces, each of them illustrating the richness of Schweitzer's thought, his sensitivities, aesthetic and moral, and the pervasive sense of calling which includes both the enrichment of his own intellect and compassion for everyone else. The books are *On the Edge of the Primeval Forest* (New York, 1923), *More From the Primeval Forest* (New York, 1931), both translated by C. T. Campion, and *African Notebook,* translated by Mrs. C. E. B. Russell (New York, 1939).

a missionary in Africa. This is not quite true. There are humbler people, who probably may not have had as much to give up, who nonetheless have absolutely forsaken friends and home for the requirements of service. Schweitzer has not done this. He has kept a sizeable house in his native Günsbach, he has never lost touch with his beloved Europe, returning every few years and sometimes for extended periods too. Again, this is not said to dispel the respect he deserves but to point out that sainthood ought not to be bestowed without knowing what the facts are. However, as one reads his literature, it becomes clear that his life is still one piece. He never pretends to give up Europe for the sake of Africa. Even on this question, he proposes to keep his interests so broad that both can be served, and this he has done with remarkable faithfulness and persistence.

III

With all of his respect for scholarship and thinking, Schweitzer still agrees with much of what our age has produced. He has been quick to criticize the pseudo-metaphysicians who have discovered energies and powers within reality which will give spiritual power to man. Schweitzer has no enthusiasm for anyone who wants to revive Platonism or Aristotelianism or who pretends to knowledge of occult agencies by which the world is run. Nowhere does he show the slightest sympathy for Hegel's philosophy or the mysteries of metaphysical idealism.

Part of his criticism of organized religion—and much of philosophy too—is that it has cultivated in believers a kind of credulity by which men credit the existence of extranatural beings and properties. Schweitzer finds it a dubious distinction in men to believe too much. Oftentimes, it is true that men believe in so many angels, so many demons, so powerful an array of non-human forces, that they conceive themselves beholden and obligated to everything but themselves. Against all of this Schweitzer is in protest. Any science, any philosophy, and any religion which multiplies the sources of authority and power, and thereby trivializes human responsibility, gets his stringent criticism. He criticizes them on both ethical-religious grounds and epistemological grounds. He claims that we neither know nor need fairies, gods, elves, gnomes, angels, and sundry other extra-terrestrial entities. Schweitzer is negative both in the interest of Christian faith, as he understands it, and also on behalf of the therapeutic use of intelligence.

Instead of all this, Schweitzer claims to be a metaphysical agnostic. Without answering every inquiry concerning such a sweeping claim, it might be well to know what Schweitzer means by it. He believes it impossible to discover a meaning in the physical universe—the universe "is" but does not "mean" anything "per se." Schweitzer enjoys the natural order, but he refuses to infer anything non-natural, supernatural, or ethical from it.

Furthermore, Schweitzer claims, as do many contemporaries, that it is impossible to establish a metaphysical or a theistic hypothesis inductively. He contends, therefore, that the supernatural claims made about Jesus of Nazareth are likewise impossible to establish on scholarly grounds. The latter point he makes in very fulsome fashion and in the context of detailed studies of primitive Christianity.

Schweitzer's agnosticism reflects a debt to Immanual Kant and surely puts him among those philosophers who are called "critical" and are somewhat anti-metaphysical. He treads a middle ground and always has seemed a little too urbane and aristocratic for those ardent majorities who believe knowledge of reality is the justification for piety and effort.

A second and distinctive feature of Schweitzer's work has been his careful delimiting of the province of historical awareness. He claims a kind of neutrality for historical knowledge that makes it compatible with the believers and unbelievers, the pros and the cons. Schweitzer's distinction is to have done this exceedingly well with research concerning the person of Jesus. Surprisingly enough, Schweitzer discovered that the picture of Jesus being offered by persons claiming to be honest historians, who dared to examine the facts, was a fiction. Liberal Protestant research was, he says, simply mistaken. Schweitzer argued that early evidence was on the side of saying Jesus believed that the world would end, that a new kingdom would be established, that He would be the new Messiah and King. Furthermore, said Schweitzer, Jesus was not the liberal persuader, the great enlightener, the gentle professorial committeeman. Instead He was somewhat imperious, authoritative, and convinced.[4]

Whether all of these views are correct or not is a matter for historians to decide, but Schweitzer's point is that the historical quest for Jesus yields no God, only a man. History cannot delineate, he contends, a figure who is either the divine and human synthesis (this because the categories would then have to include some metaphysical components) or the gentle Jesus of the liberal churches (because the facts do not warrant such a conclusion).

Schweitzer said these things a half-century ago. Some of them have become almost commonplaces among scholars. One can see easily enough, too, why Schweitzer was not always thought to be orthodox. However, whether orthodox or not, and by whatever standard, Protestant or Catholic, Schweitzer has served a great function in modern religious scholarship. He

[4]*The Quest of the Historical Jesus,* esp. pp. 396-401.

has caused intense intellectual effort among students of Scripture, and hardly a single book written in our day on these matters fails to acknowledge the importance of his work. Anyway, on these matters, Schweitzer safeguarded himself most carefully from the partisan groups. He noted that most, if not all, scholars were too confident in their belief that spiritual gain would follow from whatever historical theology could bring to the world. The orthodox here, he said, were as guilty as the liberal and critical theologians. Schweitzer contended that his task was to destroy that kind of "artifice, art, artificiality, and violence" which theologians put between men and the Gospels and, in turn, to leave the individual man alone with the sayings of Jesus.[5]

Indirectly again, Schweitzer's scholarship proposes for itself a religious task. Just as the Gospels depict a Jesus who influenced individuals by His specific words and deeds, and not by a metaphysical theory of His existence or a conception of His life as a whole, so Schweitzer argues that the effect of Biblical scholarship now is to get rid of excrescences and render us free to discover Jesus, the Savior, again.

He comes to us as One unknown, without a name, as of old, by the lakeside, He came to those men who knew Him not. He speaks to us the same word: "Follow thou me!" and sets us to the tasks which He has to fulfil for our time. He commands. And to those who obey Him, whether they be wise or simple, He will reveal Himself in the toils, the conflicts, the sufferings which they shall pass through in His fellowship, and, as an ineffable mystery, they shall learn in their own experience Who He is.[6]

[5]*Quest*, pp. 396 and 398.
[6]*Quest*, p. 401.

IV

But a third thesis is even more startling. Schweitzer argues for the independence of the ethical disposition. This independence means that an ethical suasion does not depend upon metaphysical or supernatural beliefs; and if it is asserted that they do, then there is a philosophic mistake. Admittedly this is a very difficult matter and ought not to be believed simply because it is said. Schweitzer goes on to argue that Jesus was mistaken about the immediate end of the world, but that his ethic of love is also independent of His Messianic and apocalyptic views. This means that Schweitzer does not think the Christian tradition and teaching is a seamless robe after all.

A man is, therefore, his own authorization for the good. The good can never be discovered externally. It is not a property of nature, nor of God, nor of the totality of things. The good is for Schweitzer the ethical will, and the will is ethical when it affirms existence and when it reveres the living things of the world.

I do not intend to defend this view. But Schweitzer is on the side of those who believe that the good must be postulated, not discovered; made by an act of will, not deduced from anything else.

Schweitzer is critical of Western philosophy in much the same spirit that others have been in the past century or so. He contends that most thinkers have tried to justify their optimistic ethical views by concocting an optimistic and ethical interpretation of the universe.

He does not so much quarrel with the philosophers for so doing as with their logic. For the philosophers, he contends, proceed to derive their ethic from the world-view, and obviously this is not quite the trick that it first appears to be. Even at this point Schweitzer urges a virtue upon us, viz., that of resignation. To be resigned in the presence of the universe does not mean behavorial acquiescence; instead, he tells us that we ought to be resigned cognitively, i.e., we ought to admit that we do not know, and be simultaneously energized and ethically enthusiastic.

The fourth and last point is, perhaps, contained in all the rest. Again Schweitzer makes it in a distinctive way. He contends that a man's Weltanschauung (world-view) springs from his Lebensanschauung (life-view) and not the other way around. This is as much as to say that metaphysical views are not really disinterested and are not quite what their proponents claim. Rather than finding this a criticism Schweitzer tries to show that such a grasp of world-views enhances their value.

Schweitzer is a believer in God. But true to his convictions, God is the name for the creative will which Schweitzer projects and reveres in others and nature. Without the ethical will within (which is God within, as Schweitzer understands the matter), there is no cause for talking about God in the world. But with ethical earnestness comes also a reflective disposition, and this means placing that earnestness in a context embracing as much as the mind possibly can. Schweitzer reflects, and the consequence is his world view. No one knows better than Schweitzer the limits this places upon the claims for the truth of his world view; but Schweitzer also has little interest in converting people to his world view.

And this brings us to the ethically disturbing side of this man. Early in a scholarly rich life, Schweitzer determined to discharge a debt he felt he owed the Africans. He says he wanted to atone for some of the damage the white man had done the blacks. In order to do this, he gave up those comfortable rationalizations most scholars use for their life and scholarship and began to atone for the sins of the world in his own person.

He seems to have been singularly free of the desire to convert people to his views, striking as they are, probably because he has dared to put himself under the obligation of healing the sick and of giving his own life also as a kind of ransom.

Right or wrong, Schweitzer excites thought and deserves severe argument. He has asked significant questions and served scholarship, albeit almost casually, in these later years. Certainly, he has been a good man and a reminder of the ethical potential for each of us. But more has to be said about his understanding of faith and morals before we conclude; for, whatever his personal virtues, these do not accrue to his scholarship automatically.

It appears that Schweitzer is actually a better spokesman for an ethical view of life than he is for the Christian. His enthusiasms for Goethe and for the eighteenth-century kind of philosophy cause one to wonder if he has not finally made Jesus of Nazareth a bearer of some ethical tidings, rather than distinctively New Testament teachings. To put the matter affirmatively, it is as if Schweitzer has learned to use ethical categories everywhere and always. Nothing natural or cultural is alien to his ethical enthusiasm. And, for this ethical achievement, he deserves all possible praise. Furthermore, Schweitzer is one of the most perspicuous students of ethicality in human beings that I know. Each of his books about Africa are a testimony to his sensitivity. On the one side, we see Schweitzer encompassing the termites, the diseases, the stubborn facts of the encroaching jungle, into his ethical understanding; on the other side, we watch him, almost as a detective on behalf of the human spirit, ferreting out of the most illiterate and unresponsive natives the marks of their ethical consciousness and judgments.

Schweitzer knows full-well that an ethical consciousness is

subjectively motivated by a passion within the man. No one has said more clearly than he that the ethical is invisible. Where passion, even of the moral sort, is lacking, no reflection about objective states of affairs will ever produce it. And this is how Schweitzer finally understands Jesus. The Nazarene comes to people as the stimulant to moral enthusiasm. The need for morals is more fundamental, for Schweitzer, than the need for food, shelter, and health. Preaching Jesus is a means to the end, not the end itself.

Something very noble courses through all of this. Any one who still retains vestiges of ethical earnestness cannot help respond. Surely there is a point to being reminded that everyone who enjoys his exercise of a mastery over nature must also become a servant. Moral enthusiasm has its rights and its province. Ethical enthusiasm also posits the true character of a man, and this enthusiasm is found in the doctor of Africa in an intensity approximating ideal proportions. Quite properly, too, we learn that answers to questions about the whether and whence of life are not scientific, nor can they be found by an appeal to learning of any kind, philosophical, theological, or historical. Problems of an ethical sort are human, not scholastic.

But Schweitzer allows these matters to conform his entire reflection about Christianity too. Certainly, he is one of the finest examples of personal integrity that the modern world knows, but he confuses matters considerably by refusing to specify in precise categories his convictions. He uses Christian categories to talk about enthusiasm and passion which is ethical, not Christian. Hence, too, his dismay with theology, such as he cares to discuss; for, he has little to do with specifically differentiated Christian passion and emotion. He invariably makes use of Christ and the sacraments in the interest of a kind of pathos that he admits to obtaining outside of the orbit of faith and church. No wonder then that he is not orthodox. More wonder that Christians should have sought orthodoxies in him; for few men have been as distinctively free of a conscious need for theology as he has. What Schweitzer has needed for his own self-expression he has found in Goethe; what he has needed as an external stimulant for his ethical pathos, he has found in Jesus of Nazareth.

Thus, the life and authorship of Albert Schweitzer stand before us, condemning most of us, by its strenuousness and continuity, to the awareness that we are mediocre indeed. But, there is another side too, for it is a sign of the intellectual confusion of the day, not least that of the church, that so few categories have been present by which to understand this man. Schweitzer's lasting significances as a scholar will be measured indirectly, and then only if contemporaries become clear in virtue of his pages about what it means to be ethical in contrast to what it means to be religious, and distinctively Christian. He believes that they are the same, but the scholars of modern times have shown conclusively that they are not the same. We still wait that astringent, yet passionally empathetic, analysis of Schweitzer's work, that will make it useful to our generation.

CHAPTER SIXTEEN

Everyman and Faith

Perhaps the reader who has patiently given himself to everyone of the earlier chapters now is a little weary. He might well ask— "and where does it all leave me?" Though the author cannot profess to distill the essence from every other author— as though each writer cannot do that for himself anyway—yet he can propose a few themes which belong to everyman, authors and readers alike. Amid the profuse riches that pour from the most creative minds, it is altogether too easy to forget that the glory of humanity lies in each of us equally. The things that matter most are distributed, not differentially, not as riches and talents, but as God does the rain, on the just and the unjust, on all without discrimination. The differences between the learned and the learners, the scholars and the students, the authors and the readers, the clerics and the laity, begin to fade into insignificance when the likenesses are considered.

In what follows faith will be considered from another vantage point. It may even seem that the older point of view, one hallowed by tradition and holy association, is being given stature once again. This is surely true. When all the advances of learning are trumpeted through the world, when everyone heralds the dawn of a new day and everything old seems about to be vanquished, it is salutary to remember that there is still room for faith. Furthermore, nothing else ever quite fills that room, no matter how new, how bold, or how profound.

These things are said not to disparage learning or to discourage a student. On the contrary, there is no substitute whatsoever for learning. However, it is still true that learning does not displace faith nor faith learning. So, granted all of the relations to faith which reflection about being, about psychoanalysis, about history and other subjects, might reveal, there is no ground in all of this for suggesting that the learned man has any religious advantage over the unlearned. His advantages remain to the end only intellectual. Unlike the affairs of the world, where a few accidental occurrences sometimes make a man great in the eyes of his fellows, learning never compounds itself into faith. Learning, in fact, never becomes anything else. Though some seekers might be disappointed to discover this, it is incumbent not to ask too much of scholarship and science. The person who is content with what learning can bring has already learned not to expect the Kingdom of Heaven as a consequence of teaching, but, contrariwise, neither can he expect faith to give him the explanations of the mechanisms of nature or of the ways of nations. Faith and learning have their limits and proprieties. When considering these, we can both rejoice in our common propensity for faith and enjoy our differential talents for culture and learning.

Modern scholarship has served the ethical and religious interests of men very well. The cure for bad objectivity is a more precisely stipulated mode of objectivity. The latter is coming about in the contemporary world and Christians have everything to gain in such a development. For, with even the modest success that we can note to date in several areas of scholarship, it is becoming increasingly clear that there is an autonomy to ethical and religious decision, even faith. Just as the world itself permits a kind of freedom, so, too, does knowledge of the world permit freedom. Like the stars which may incline but do not determine, so knowledge may incline but it does not finally dispose our wills nor command our spirits. By the same token, it permits the pursuit of knowledge for its own sake.

II

One of the ever-present temptations of thought is to give more significance to the large cosmos around us than to the small cosmos within. Undoubtedly each of us knows both of these and can distinguish one from the other. It almost seems a perfection in a man to escape his inner life and its purposings, its dismaying limitations, its parochialisms and privacies, in order to exult in the intellectual grasp of the externalities in which we live. To think appears as an escape from the inner cosmos to the outer cosmos, the world around us.

Something can be said for this point of view. Part of what is meant by detachment and disinterestedness is precisely the achievement of freedom and emancipation from the delimiting conditions of our own subjectivity. However, it is also in order to be always reminded that we have firsthand contact only with our inner cosmos. This is ours to know intimately and well. Any relationship which we have to the cosmos around us is conjectural and secondhand, indirect and mediated. Knowledge of the world, other than ourselves, is always hypothetical.

In fact, the matter can be pushed even further. The inner life is for most of us a somewhat random series of happenings, of impulses and drives, of chaotic energies and enthusiasms. Initially it is not a cosmos, but a chaos. It needs ordering and orientation. But any principle which brings system has to be applied from within. Only by a decision, daily renewed and constantly brought to bear upon all that we are, is character formed and the inner life disciplined. There is no mass production of character. Each man is still the guardian of the springs of his own character and alone has access to those motives which make him distinctively human.

Most of the learning in the world is about the large cosmos in which we find ourselves. All of us seem to be guided by a loose conviction to the effect that the world is a cosmos, an order, rather than a chaos. In one way or another, the pictures of existence allowed us by knowledge never quite disconfirm nor confirm this genial view. Vast numbers of orderly and lawful sequences have been discovered in the events to which man is a spectator, and together these strengthen the long-standing view that the world is an ordered whole.

A quixotic view, hovering over men almost since the beginning of learning, has been to the effect that the decision about the inner life would be aided materially if we only knew what principle or principles of order obtained in the large order. Learning has almost invariably fanned this flickering hope of men into a major flame. The indecision and uncertainty that all of us must acknowledge about how we should ourselves be, promises to disappear if only we can discover what makes the diversity around us an universe.

Faith has often been defined as a by-product and learning has been deemed a kind of broker, justifying a decision by showing that the entire world is dependent upon the same principle. However, if what we have read is the case, there are several limitations to be considered. There is nowadays no single system of order acknowledged by all of the branches of learning. Crudely, this means that the hypotheses and principles achieved in a limited area of learning cannot be extended today to all frames of learning. So we are no longer able to use scientific and scholarly evidence to characterize the world around us as a cosmos. There simply is no evidence available now for characterizing the totality of things according to any single set of rules or principles. There are, instead, many sets of laws, and each of them applies to a limited number of phenomena.

Thus any attempt to infer what ought to be the principle governing one's inner life from the principle governing the universe is vitiated at the beginning. There is no established way of saying what that principle is which makes the world around us orderly.

Furthermore, there are no available ways of deducing from the regimen of the cosmos the regimen of our inner life. Any attempt to state how and why this must be done is an instance of blatant dogmatism. It makes as bad science as it does ethics to propose that the transition from one to another is a matter facilitated by learning and made necessary by insight. Protestations have come on this point from historians, from moralists, from logicians, from cosmologists and numerous others, some of them already canvassed in these pages.

The qualitative distinction which can be drawn between the rules and principles by which the workings of nature and history are explained and those by which a man must govern and judge his life also warrants our saying that the transition between the two kinds is not logical nor inferential. Contemporary theory about this says that one cannot deduce an "ought" from an "is," a "value" from a "fact," a "faith" from an "hypothesis."

For the moment these details are not decisive. It is most important to recognize the autonomy and rights of the inner life, with which each of us has legitimate concern. That we cannot make the latter a product of the former seems clear enough. Faith is actually a way to give purpose, or what philosophers and theologians call teleology, to the inner life. Every endeavor to be a Christian man requires a decision, an intent, a purpose, a wish, an act, by which it can be effected. By such menial and small beginnings, grace takes hold of each of us in turn.

Modern learning has not disclosed the teleology of the cosmos to us. Despite the advances of learning, that large teleology escapes us. If it is there, it is not apparent to us in our detachment and disinterested gaze. In fact, the teleology in the universe seems to be there only if it is in the man who looks at the universe. So, again, the confidences sustained by the hope that more learning would make the purposings of God more apparent have been shattered. But this means nothing more than that faith is still ours to have. We can purpose the ways of God for ourselves and can understand the world in the light of all that makes our inner life rich and purposeful. Instead of faith being vanquished it seems rather that faith has its province, wherein it is sovereign and subject to nothing alien.

Manifestly this is to make everyman's inner life as important as anyone else's. Though not everyone can scan the heavens and know what makes the behavior of things as it is, there is no ground for assuming that this disadvantage is one unto eternal life. No, we must stop short and admit that God is no respecter of persons, or, instead, that God respects each man equally. Access to faith is access via one's inner life and the Scripture and not the cosmos around us. This is both the demonstration of learning and the testimony of holy writ.

III

But another conclusion is also open to us at this juncture. Two kinds of perfection are available to everyman. On the one side, we can both deplore and destroy our ignorance; on the other side, we can also refashion and reconstitute our interests. These two processes, for this is what they are, are independent of one another, both in act and in effect.

The intellectual life surely has its glories. These are bountifully attested to by men of culture and learning. That it is more proper and just to be learned than ignorant seems hardly an arguable thesis. Everyone who is a teacher is dedicated to the destruction of human ignorance. One of the awesome and symptomatic facts about human beings is that their ignorance is limitless, boundless and all-encompassing upon the occasion of birth. If people want to be born, they apparently must be born ignorant. All the teachers in the world, professional and otherwise, are dedicated to the task of overcoming this feature of human nativity. Every individual moves from abysmal ignorance to some kind of knowledge. Not only is it necessary that he do so in order to stay alive, but there is a kind of perfection which is achieved in arriving at a knowledgeable estate. There is an unanimity among men on the fact that knowledge is an object of legitimate desire and a kind of good.

However, men are also born with tractable wills. Human malleability is another pervasive fact about the newly born. This fact makes every individual subject to all kinds of persuasions and pressures. Because our interests are never completely shaped at birth, we are potentially good or bad. In at least one significant sense, we are neither one with decisiveness at the hour of our birth. Even if one admits that sin is present at our origin, as original as each individual, still this does not deny the adaptability of the ethical will as much as it suggests the kind of limitations which do obtain.

Very few of the interests which we have as young people are sufficiently resilient and meaning-laden to remain long with us. One by one they are replaced or integrated into larger patterns of concern and commitment. Ethical perfection is a matter largely of ordering and acquiring interests which are durable and relevant to the vicissitudes of our lives. Conflicts of interest are real and the romance of human living is well told by the endeavors to be consistently ordered to a single love and steadfastly given to those things which matter most. Moral degeneracy is illustrated both by having no interests and sinking into apathy and disconcern and by having several or many interests and being torn by indecision or disloyalty to the objects of human care.

Again, however, the boundaries of faith are made clear to us. For faith is also a human perfection. But it is a perfection that climaxes the moral life. Luther loved to reiterate a view first stated in the New Testament, namely, that the moral law was a kind of schoolmaster leading, even driving, us to faith. Modern learning surely has no rights to any pretention on this score. Learning is a perfection, but its perfection is limited and aristocratic, open only to those who have the plentiful abilities to achieve knowledge in place of their ignorance. Faith is a perfection open to anyone who can repent of his moral life and vagaries of interest. And everyone can do this.

One perfection never becomes the other either. Just as there is a distinction in point of departure, so there is a difference in the point of arrival. From ignorance we can move to knowledge; from the lack of interest or a kind of interest, we can move to another interest. But, an interest or a concern does not directly make one intelligent any more than does intelligence about any matter whatsoever necessarily and automatically create an interest.

Faith is, as Paul Tillich has so nobly said, a matter of ultimate concern. And concern is not created by the world and things in it. Faith is a perfection open to those who are either intellectually perfect or intellectually imperfect or somewhere in between. Faith is for the ignorant and the intelligent providing that they care about their own salvation and good. If they care enough, enough to revoke and to repent their present state, whatever their degree of cognitive understanding, they then can be perfected as God sees fit.

This is not a repudiation of the intellectual life. For a man of faith may also be a man of talent. Perchance he too wants and needs the perfection of knowing. But if he achieves it, he does it not because it is the means to the perfection of faith, but, rather, because it is an incremental factor in his own life for which he must also give account.

IV

Lastly and still another way to consider our faith—the highest reaches of the intellectual life are achieved when students learn how to justify the views which they hold about matters of fact. For it is not enough to have views; it is also necessary to know what makes them justifiable. Many people learn all kinds of things laid down by others. But the sign of superficiality which gives them away is that often such people cannot show why a proposition ought to be believed. When men speak of the warrantability of a sentence they mean to indicate that there are grounds for asserting the sentence to be true about some matter of fact.

The justification of our language is a part, and a very significant one, of the large responsibility of being knowledgeable. The difference between the person who speaks in a justified manner, where facts and the rules of inference permit him so to speak, and the one who does not so speak, is a very large and important one. But it is, nonetheless, not as large as the distinction between a man whose speech is justified and one whose life is justified.

For withal, everyman is also in business to justify his own existence, to quiet his anxious conscience and to make himself morally acceptable. One of Kierkegaard's pseudonymous authors says that life itself is an examination in which men cannot cheat. If one tries to understand what the New Testament's story is about, surely a quick and encompassing answer is that it concerns the justification of men's lives and not of their views. Furthermore, the Bible claims that men are wrong if they believe that they can actually justify themselves. It is almost as if it suggests that the concern about justification is legitimate but that the common resolutions are illegitimate.

Suffice it to say again that all the intellection of which men are capable, that of even the finest of intellects, does not assuage by a whit their troubled judgment of themselves. This is even said by the authors we have encountered in this book. For not a one of them has established the thesis that a true view or the thinking of a true view by a man is enough to make him good rather than bad, justified rather than unjustified. Instead it seems almost as if modern learning is an indirect apologetic for the Christian faith. By making clear that learning and evidence justifies nothing but a view about something or other, it leaves wide open the question of how it is that men are justified. Not even the learning about God, about the Bible, about Jesus, is the same as faith.

The sickening human realization that one's life is not all that it ought to be cannot be relieved by more reflection. If anything, more thought will make the realization more vivid and the agony more acute. And, granted the ability that some have to know the truth about almost anything one pleases, still there is nothing in all of the justified views any more than in the unjustified ones which will provoke human redemption.

This is a part of what the French call "la condition humaine," the human condition. It is a testimony to modern learning, in contradistinction to some of the earlier periods of intellectual history, that that human situation is now exceedingly well described. In fact it is now so clear that the role of faith can be clearly seen, more clearly perhaps than ever before. However, to see the role of faith is still not to play it.

V

In a beautiful passage in one of his philosophic books Kierkegaard depicts an old man speaking to a grandson at the graveside of the father. Both were dressed in mourning clothes as they sat by the freshly dug grave. The old man addressed himself to the boy:

> He told him that there was a wisdom which tried to fly beyond faith, that on the other side of faith there was a wide stretch of country like the blue mountains, an illusory land, which to a mortal eye might appear to yield a certainty higher than that of faith; but the believer feared this mirage, as the sailor fears a similar appearance on the sea; that it was an illusion of eternity in which a mortal cannot live, but only lose his faith when he permits his gaze to be fascinated by the sight.[1]

Kierkegaard's reflections on the old man and his sadness are pertinent to everything said in this book.

> The venerable old man with his faith seemed to be an individual with an absolutely justified grievance, a man whom existence had mistreated, because a modern speculation, like a change in the currency, had made property values in the realm of faith insecure.[2]

[1]Soren Kierkegaard, *Concluding Unscientific Postscript*, translated by D. F. Swenson (Princeton, 1941), p. 213.
[2]*Op. cit.*, pp. 213-214.

The confusion of the old man's son Kierkegaard likens to that of the entire age. Faith is assumed, he says, to be something that can be directly communicated and objectively appropriated. This misunderstanding he also explains:

> It must, in short, doubtless be rooted in the fact that on account of our vastly increased knowledge, men had forgotten what it means to EXIST and what INWARD-NESS signifies.[3]

It must be apparent already that God contrives to maintain His invisibility. Not even the most refined tools of learning have enabled us to discern the presence of God. Nature is His handiwork and history His arena, but only the handiwork and the arena are directly present. But all of this is to say again that within everyman is another potentiality, not of sight and hearing and learning, but of moral sensitivity and ethical inwardness. When this inner life is awakened and becomes strong, then the relationship to God is established. Then it also becomes possible to see God everywhere. This is the work and province of faith.

[3]*Op. cit.*, p. 216.

Index